COOKS FOR
KOSOVO

Great recipes from Britain's favourite TV cooks

COMPILED AND INTRODUCED BY SOPHIE GRIGSON

To Bridget,
via Jennie,

from

Sophie Grigson

HEADLINE

First published in 1999
by HEADLINE BOOK PUBLISHING

10 9 8 7 6 5 4 3 2 1

ISBN 0 7472 7139 9

Book design by Design/Section

Printed in the UK by Butler & Tanner, London and Frome, Somerset

HEADLINE BOOK PUBLISHING
A division of the Hodder Headline Group
338 Euston Road
London NW1 3BH

www.headline.co.uk
www.hodderheadline.com

Please note:
In order to speed up production, we have unfortunately had to cut a few corners, the most notable being that we simply did not have time to harmonise the formats of all the recipes and check the changes back with the contributors. They are presented more or less as they arrived at the Headline offices, which means that users of the book will find some inconsistencies in style from page to page. Apologies and thank you for your indulgence. **Sophie Grigson**

℣ indicates vegetarian dishes

Introduction by
Sophie Grigson

Night after night, I watched those awful scenes of homeless people streaming over the borders of Kosovo in desperate search for some kind of safety. Families that had been torn apart, children who had lost not just their homes, but often their closest relations, the bewildered weary despair of those men and women who had made it to the overcrowded refugee camps, but whose lives had been shattered, all this was almost too much to take in. Like so many others in Britain, I could hardly bear to turn on the news, but it wasn't a situation that could be ignored from the comfort of my home.

This collection of recipes is one small way that I and my fellow television cooks and chefs could make some contribution towards alleviating the horrifying effects of hatred and war upon innocent civilians. Of course, now the fighting seems to have come to an end, and slowly Kosovar Albanians are trickling back to their towns and villages, but their plight is not over. It will take years to put back some sort of infrastructure, years to repair homes, years to heal the wounds, years to mend lives, years to ease the pain.

It would be all too easy now to ignore calls for donations to the Kosovo Crisis Appeal, but quite wrong. Money is still desperately needed to feed and clothe people, to treat the ill, and to help the refugees rebuild their lives. One way you can help is by buying this book – £1 will go to the Appeal for every copy sold. So go out and buy more, give them to your friends and family, and encourage them to do the same.

Disasters **Emergency** Committee
Working together

The Kosovo Crisis Appeal

When people see harrowing images of human suffering on their television screens they want to know how they can do something to help. Sometimes the answer can be found on those same television screens when a national appeal is launched by the Disasters Emergency Committee, or the DEC as it is more commonly known.

The DEC was established in 1966 to help coordinate the response of aid agencies to overseas disasters. It has launched over forty appeals since then on behalf of its members which include household names like Oxfam, the British Red Cross, Save the Children and Help the Aged.

The aim of the DEC is to save lives and help bring effective and timely relief to those in greatest need. That is why, on 6 April 1999, we responded to the desperate plight of refugees from Kosovo by launching the Kosovo Crisis Appeal. In the ten or so weeks since then the appeal has raised over £40 million, a remarkable sign of public compassion and generosity.

The money is a huge help to the aid agencies working with refugees throughout the region but much more remains to be done, especially now the war has ended and people are beginning to return home to a land laid desolate. Homes have been burned down, whole villages destroyed. The people will somehow have to rebuild their lives and communities. They have the spirit to do this, but they will need help from the outside world – they will need our help, for many months to come.

Jamie McCaul
Executive Secretary
Disasters Emergency Committee

French Onion Soup

Serves 6

1½ lb (700g) onions, thinly sliced

2 tablespoons olive oil

2 oz (50g) butter

2 cloves garlic, crushed

½ teaspoon granulated sugar

2 pints (1.2 litres) good beef stock

10 fl oz (275ml) dry white wine

2 tablespoons Cognac

salt and freshly milled black pepper

For the croûtons

French bread or *baguettine*, cut into 1 inch (2.5cm) diagonal slices

1 tablespoon olive oil

1-2 cloves garlic, crushed

To serve

6 large or 12 small croûtons

8 oz (225g) Gruyère, grated

Delia Smith

There are few things more comforting than making a real French Onion Soup – slowly cooked caramelized onions that turn mellow and sweet in a broth laced with white wine and Cognac. The whole thing is finished off with crunchy baked croûtons of crusty bread topped with melted, toasted cheese. If ever there was a winter stomach warmer, this is surely it!

Preheat the oven to 180°C/350°F/Gas Mark 4. You will also need a heavy based saucepan or flameproof casserole of 6-pint (3.5-litre) capacity and a heatproof tureen or soup bowls.

First make the croûtons – begin by drizzling the olive oil on a large, solid baking sheet, add the crushed garlic and, then, using your hands, spread the oil and garlic all over the baking sheet. Now place the bread slices on top of the oil, then turn over each one so that both sides have been lightly coated with the oil. Bake for 20-25 minutes till crisp and crunchy.

4

Next, place the saucepan or casserole on a high heat and melt the oil and butter together. When this is very hot, add the onions, garlic and sugar, and keep turning them from time to time until the edges of the onions have turned dark – this will take about 6 minutes. Then reduce the heat to its lowest setting and leave the onions to carry on cooking very slowly for about 30 minutes, by which time the base of the pan will be covered with a rich, nut brown, caramelized film.

After that pour in the stock and white wine, season, then stir with a wooden spoon, scraping the base of the pan well. As soon as it all comes up to simmering point, turn down the heat to its lowest setting, then go away and leave it to cook very gently, without a lid, for about 1 hour.

All this can be done in advance, but when you're ready to serve the soup, bring it back up to simmering point, taste to check for seasoning – and if it's extra-cold outside, add a couple of tablespoons of Cognac! Warm the tureen or soup bowls in a low oven and pre-heat the grill to its highest setting. Then ladle in the hot soup and top with the croûtons, allowing them to float on the top of the soup.

Now sprinkle the grated Gruyère thickly over the croûtons and place the whole lot under the grill until the cheese is golden brown and bubbling. Serve immediately – and don't forget to warn your guests that everything is very hot!

Crab Cocktail

Serves 4-6

400-450g (14-16 oz) crabmeat
(white and brown)
225ml (8 fl oz) mayonnaise
1 shallot, very finely chopped
2 teaspoons Dijon mustard
1 tablespoon tomato purée
2 teaspoons chopped fresh tarragon
Tabasco sauce
4-6 crisp lettuce leaves,
e.g. Cos or Webb's
1 tablespoon vinaigrette dressing
salt and freshly ground pepper

To serve
lemon wedges
brown bread and butter or toast

Sophie Grigson

Crab cocktail has been out of fashion for a decade or more but I'm delighted that it has now come back with a vengeance. I've always loved it: when made with fresh crab and good mayonnaise, spiked with a hint of tarragon, it is one of the most sublime first courses.

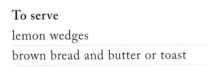

Flake any large bits of white crabmeat. Mix the mayonnaise with the shallot, mustard, tomato purée, tarragon, a few shakes of Tabasco to taste and salt and pepper. Stir about three-quarters into the crab. Taste, and add the rest if you think it needs it (the mixture should be very rich and quite sloppy), then balance the seasoning.

Just before serving, shred the lettuce leaves and toss with the vinaigrette. Divide between individual plates and top with the crab mayonnaise. Serve with lemon wedges and brown bread and butter, or toast.

Pea and Coriander Soup ♈

Darina Allen

Serves 6

55g (2 oz) butter
140g (5 oz) onion, finely chopped
2 cloves garlic, peeled and chopped
1 green chilli, deseeded and finely chopped
450g (1 lb) peas (good-quality frozen are fine)
900ml (1½ pints) homemade vegetable stock
2 tablespoons chopped fresh coriander
salt, freshly ground pepper and sugar

For the garnish
softly whipped cream
fresh coriander leaves

This utterly delicious soup has a perky zing with the addition of fresh chilli.

Melt the butter on a gentle heat and sweat the onion, garlic and chilli for 3-4 minutes. Add the peas and cover with the stock. Bring to the boil and simmer for 7-8 minutes. Add the coriander and liquidise. Season with salt, freshly ground pepper and a pinch of sugar, which enhances the flavour even further.

Serve with a swirl of softly whipped cream and a few fresh coriander leaves sprinkled over the top.

STARTERS

Mussel and Saffron Soup

Serves 6

1.5kg (3 lb) fresh mussels

600ml (1 pint) dry white wine

50g (2 oz) butter

2 leeks, cleaned and finely chopped

2 sticks celery, finely chopped

1 carrot, peeled and finely chopped

2 cloves garlic, finely chopped

a good pinch of saffron stamens

600ml (1 pint) double cream

cayenne pepper

Maldon salt

2 tablespoons finely chopped fresh chives

Nick Nairn

You need two things

for success here: good

fat mussels and real

saffron stamens.

Scrub the mussels well and pull out the beards protruding from between the two closed shells. Discard any that won't close when they are lightly tapped on the work surface.

Heat a large pan over a high heat. Bung in the mussels and the white wine, cover and cook, shaking the pan occasionally for 3-4 minutes or until the mussels have opened. Discard any that stay closed.

Tip the mussels into a colander set over a large bowl or another pan and then pass the cooking liquor once more through a very fine sieve and reserve it. Set aside half of the mussels and remove the meats from the remainder.

Melt the butter in the pan you used for the mussels, add the chopped vegetables and the garlic and cook over a medium-high heat for a few minutes. Add the reserved mussel liquor and the saffron and leave to simmer for 10 minutes.

Add the cream and bring the soup back to the boil. Add the mussel meats and mussels in their shells, cayenne pepper and a little salt if needed and simmer for about a minute until the mussels have heated through. Stir in the chopped chives, spoon the soup into warmed bowls and serve straightaway.

Salad of Watermelon, Feta and Toasted Pumpkin Seeds ♈

Serves 6

1 cup (150g/5oz) pumpkin seeds
60ml (2 fl oz) extra virgin olive oil
1.5kg (3¼ lb) watermelon
300g (11 oz) sheep's feta
crushed black pepper
3 juicy lemons

Peter Gordon

As far as I know this salad has its roots in Israel. We serve it a lot at the Sugar Club, and though people are at first intrigued by the combination – finding it a little weird – they soon learn to love it.

Preheat the oven to 180°C/350°F/Gas 4.

Mix the pumpkin seeds with 20ml (¾ fl oz) olive oil, spread on a baking sheet and toast in the oven for 8-12 minutes until golden. Don't burn.

Cut the watermelon into chunks and peel it. If you have time remove the seeds, but it's not essential.

Slice or crumble the feta over the watermelon, sprinkle with the toasted seeds and crushed pepper, drizzle with olive oil and serve with lemon wedges. Delicious!

Curried Cream of Cauliflower Soup with Coriander Purée ♈

Serves 4

1 large cauliflower, cut into small florets

1 small onion, peeled and coarsely chopped

1 teaspoon curry powder

2 tablespoons groundnut oil

200ml (7 fl oz) whipping cream or milk

salt and freshly ground black pepper

For the coriander purée

1 small bunch of fresh coriander

50ml (2 fl oz) groundnut oil

juice of ½ lemon

To serve

2 tablespoons groundnut oil mixed with ¼ teaspoon curry powder

1 tablespoon coriander seeds, lightly crushed if you like

Raymond Blanc

As this soup may be served hot or cold, you can make it a day or so in advance. Make the coriander purée at the last moment or it will discolour.

Sweat the chopped onion with the curry powder in the groundnut oil for 2 minutes, then add the cauliflower florets and cook over a medium heat for 3 minutes. Cover with water and boil for 10-12 minutes until the cauliflower is totally soft. Add water if necessary during the cooking time to keep the cauliflower covered.

Add the cream and liquidise everything in a blender until smooth. Season well and set aside.

For the coriander purée, purée the coriander, leaves and stalks, oil and lemon juice together in a mortar and pestle or small blender, then season to taste.

To serve, heat the soup gently, then pour into bowls and spoon over the coriander purée and curry oil. Sprinkle with the coriander seeds and serve.

Mixed Mediterranean Salad

Ainsley Harriott

Serves 4

25g (1 oz) butter

4 tablespoons olive oil

2 whole garlic cloves

2 slices white bread, preferably from an uncut loaf, cut into 1cm (½ in) cubes for croûtons

400g (14 oz) can artichoke hearts, drained and halved

4 rashers streaky bacon or 4 slices pancetta

200g (7 oz) packet mixed salad leaves

1 tablespoon snipped fresh chives

I love this starter with its fresh tastes and vibrant colours from the Mediterranean.

For the dressing

6 tablespoons fresh lemon juice

8 tablespoons olive oil

3 tablespoons crème fraîche

50g (2 oz) feta cheese, crumbled

freshly ground black pepper

Make the dressing: whisk together the lemon juice and oil. Gradually add the crème fraîche, feta cheese and black pepper.

Heat the butter and oil in a frying pan over a low heat, add the garlic and cook for a few minutes, then remove garlic.

Increase the heat, add the cubes of bread and fry until golden brown. Remove the croûtons with a slotted spoon, then drain well on kitchen paper.

Add the artichoke hearts to the same frying pan and fry for about 2 minutes until golden and crispy on the outside.

Grill the bacon until it is crisp, then crumble it into pieces. Arrange the salad leaves on four large serving plates. Divide the artichoke hearts and croûtons among the plates, then spoon over the dressing.

Sprinkle over the crispy bacon and top with chives and black pepper.

Fresh Goat's Cheese with Hedgerow Herbs ♈

Serves 6 as a starter or cheese course

about 500g (1 lb) very fresh soft goat's cheese

salt and freshly ground black pepper

Small bunches each of:

chives

wild garlic leaves

wild chervil (young cow parsley)

bittercress or watercress

You can add or substitute home-grown or shop-bought herbs:

parsley

chervil

garlic

tarragon

To serve with the cheese

batons of carrot and celery, whole radishes and other crudités

fresh crusty bread

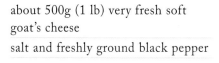

Hugh Fearnley-Whittingstall

Mixing very fresh goat's cheese with garlic and herbs is a French tradition, and it's often served as a starter with crusty bread and crudités.

Wash, shake dry, and finely chop all the herbs. Add three-quarters of the chopped herbs to the goat's cheese in a bowl. If you don't have wild garlic, crush a garlic clove and add that to the bowl.

Mix the herbs and cheese well together with a wooden spoon or fork. Season to taste with salt and freshly ground black pepper.

Sprinkle the remaining herbs over the top of the cheese and take the bowl to the table with the bread and crudités.

Serve with a good rosé or chilled Beaujolais.

Crispy Wontons

Makes about 6

110g (4 oz) raw prawns

350g (12 oz) minced pork

2 teaspoons salt

1 teaspoon freshly ground black pepper

2 tablespoons finely chopped garlic

3 tablespoons finely chopped spring onions

2 tablespoons fish sauce or light soy sauce

1 teaspoon sugar

3 tablespoons finely chopped fresh coriander

1 egg, lightly beaten

225g (8 oz) wonton skins

400ml (14 fl oz) groundnut (peanut) oil,
for deep-frying

For the spicy dipping sauce (nam prik pla)

2-3 small fresh red Thai chillies,
seeded and sliced

1 tablespoon sugar

3 tablespoons fish sauce or light soy sauce

3 tablespoons lime juice

2 teaspoons water

Ken Hom

These savoury wontons are familiar to lovers of Chinese food, who will also note that these crispy delights are subtly changed by a Thai flavour.

Peel the prawns and discard the shells. Using a small sharp knife, remove the fine digestive cord. Wash them in cold water, rinse and pat dry with kitchen paper. Coarsely chop.

Put the prawns and pork in a large bowl, add the salt and pepper and mix well, either by kneading with your hand or by stirring with a wooden spoon. Then add the rest of the filling ingredients, down to and including the egg, and stir well. Wrap the bowl with clingfilm and chill it for 20 minutes.

In a small bowl, combine all the ingredients for the sauce. Set aside.

To stuff the wontons, put 1 tablespoon of the filling in the centre of the first wonton skin. Dampen the edges with a little water and bring up the sides around the filling. Pinch the edges together at the top so that the wonton is sealed. Repeat until you have used up all the filling.

Heat the oil in a deep-fat fryer or a large wok until it is hot. Deep-fry the wontons, a few at a time, for 3 minutes or until golden and crispy. Drain the wontons well on kitchen paper. Serve immediately with the dipping sauce.

Shakshouka ♈

Serves 4

3 tablespoons olive oil

2 green peppers, thinly sliced

1 onion, chopped

3 garlic cloves, crushed

salt

1 teaspoon paprika

1 large pinch cayenne pepper

1 teaspoon ground cumin

4 tomatoes, sliced

4 eggs

Claudia Roden

A popular dish all

over the Arab

world. Serve hot as

an appetizer or as a

light meal.

Heat the olive oil in a large frying pan and fry the peppers and the onion until they are soft – about 10 minutes.

Add the garlic and, as soon as it begins to brown, a pinch of salt and the spices and stir well.

Add the tomatoes and stir gently.

Make four hollows in the mixture with the back of a spoon. Break the eggs into the hollows and cook gently until they are set – about 8 minutes.

STARTERS

Tomato, Mozzarella and Basil Terrine ♈

Serves 4

12-14 large ripe plum tomatoes
500g (18 oz) mozzarella cheese
a large bunch of fresh basil
salt and freshly ground black pepper
4 sprigs fresh basil
good olive oil and balsamic vinegar

Anton Mosimann

A colourful, fresh starter that is perfect for summer entertaining.

Cut the plum tomatoes to fit a small, deep terrine dish. Hold a tomato upright, stem uppermost, and cut down thick slices off the four sides, leaving a square core in the middle (discard this). This will give you four roughly rectangular 1.5cm (½ inch) thick slices. Cut all the tomatoes similarly. Flatten the slices gently under the palm of your hand and trim into neat rectangles.

Cut the mozzarella cheese into similar slices, and trim into neat rectangles.

Wash, gently pat dry, and pick off the basil leaves. Line the terrine with clingfilm. Place a layer of sliced tomatoes, skin side down, into the base of the terrine. Try to make the slices fit exactly to give a neat final effect.

Season well and add a layer of mozzarella slices, followed by a layer of basil leaves. Keep adding layers in the same order, finishing with a layer of tomato.

Cover with clingfilm and a flat piece of card cut to fit the top of the terrine exactly. Place a light weight on top and chill for several hours. This will help the layers stick together.

To serve, unmould carefully on to a chopping board, and slice into thick individual slices.

Use the fresh basil, olive oil and balsamic vinegar to garnish each plate.

Roast Vine Tomato, Aged Balsamic and New Season Olive Oil ♈

Serves 4

1 ciabatta loaf
1 clove garlic
75ml (2½ fl oz) new season olive oil
4 sprigs cherry tomatoes on the vine
sea salt
black pepper
1 bunch basil
15ml (½ fl oz) aged balsamic vinegar

Andrew Sargent

This dish is so simple

to make yet tastes

and looks delicious.

Slice the ciabatta into 4 thin pieces lengthways, rub with the garlic clove, drizzle with a little olive oil and grill until golden.

Place the tomatoes still on the vine in a baking tray, drizzle with a little olive oil, and season with salt and pepper. Place in a hot oven (220°C/425°F/Gas 7) and cook for 4 minutes.

Place a slice of ciabatta on the plate, with a vine of the warm tomatoes on top. Tear the basil and sprinkle over. Drizzle with the remainder of the olive oil and finish with the balsamic.

STARTERS

Glazed Chilli Quail with Bok Choy

Serves 4

4 quail or poussin, split in half through
the breastbone

1 head bok choy, trimmed and sliced

½ red pepper, cut into fine strips

2 spring onions, finely sliced

Paul and Jeanne Rankin

*Quail is finger-licking
food and is at its best
cooked on the bone. If
you can't find quail,
poussin is a good
alternative.*

For the marinade

2 tablespoons dark soy sauce

2 tablespoons brown sugar

3 tablespoons chilli sauce

1 tablespoon chopped ginger

1 tablespoon sherry

1 clove garlic crushed

1 tablespoon vegetable oil

1 teaspoon toasted sesame oil (optional)

The day before, combine all the marinade ingredients in a ceramic
bowl. Toss the quail or poussin in the marinade, cover, and refrigerate
overnight.

Preheat the grill to high. Remove the birds from the marinade, and
place skin side down on a baking sheet. Place under the grill on a low
shelf, and cook for 5 minutes for quail and 5-10 minutes longer for
poussin. Turn the birds over, and cook for another 5-7 minutes for
quail and 5-10 minutes longer (or until cooked) for poussin, basting
occasionally with the marinade. Meanwhile, bring a pot of salted water
to the boil and blanch the bok choy and the pepper for 1 minute.
Drain well, and toss thoroughly in 2 tablespoons of the marinade.
Arrange this into a bed on warmed plates, and place the quail or
poussin halves on top. Garnish with the finely sliced spring onions
scattered over the top.

Thai Green Chicken Curry

Serves 4

1-2 tablespoons Thai green curry paste

2 tablespoons vegetable oil

2 large cloves garlic, mashed to a paste with a little salt

2 stems lemongrass, tender part only, finely chopped

2 lime leaves, shredded

750ml (1¼ pints) coconut milk

4 tablespoons chopped coriander, leaves and tender stalks

12 chicken thighs, skin removed

2-3 green chillies, seeded and finely chopped

4 tablespoons ripped basil leaves

2 tablespoons *nam pla* (fish sauce)

1 tablespoon freshly squeezed lime juice

Antony Worrall Thompson

I am really into the smooth silky taste of this very easy curry.

Fry the curry paste (the more you add, the hotter it will be) in the vegetable oil over a high heat for 3 minutes. Add the garlic, lemongrass, lime leaves and half the coconut milk and cook until the sauce starts to split, about 5 minutes.

Add the coriander, chicken and chilli and simmer for 15 minutes. Add the remaining coconut milk and cook for a further 5 minutes.

Just before serving fold in the basil leaves, fish sauce and lime juice. Serve with fragrant rice and garnish with extra coriander leaves.

Slow-honey-roast Duck

Serves 2

Gary Rhodes

1.25-1.5kg (2½-3 lb) oven-ready duck

1 teaspoon crushed white peppercorns

1 dessertspoon coarse sea salt

5 heaped tablespoons clear honey

The flavours from this dish remind me of the taste found in Chinese pancakes with spring onions and cucumber. The duck is so tender and gives a very full flavour, which makes you just want to eat more and more of it.

Preheat the oven to 160°C/325°F/Gas 3. The duck-breast skin should first be scored four or five times, just cutting into the skin itself. Put the duck in a small roasting tray. Sprinkle the peppercorns over the duck with the salt, pushing the salt onto the skin. Spoon the honey over the duck, making sure it is completely covered. Place the duck in the oven.

After the first half hour, baste the duck with the honey and duck residue in the roasting tray. Leave to slow-roast for a further 30 minutes. The salt sprinkled over the duck will draw the excess water and fat from the skin itself and this will obviously collect in the roasting tray. After the second half hour, remove the duck from the roasting tray and carefully, from one corner, pour off as much excess fat as possible; it will be sitting on top of the honey in the tray. Replace the duck in the tray, baste with the honey residue and return to the oven. The duck can now be left to slow-roast, basting every 15 minutes for a further hour.

The duck has now been slowly cooked for 2 hours. Remove the duck once more from the tray and again pour off any excess fat. Baste the duck with the honey and return to the oven.

During the last half hour of cooking, baste the duck every 5-10 minutes. The honey will now have reduced and become very thick, glazing the duck even more. After the 2½ hours are up, remove the duck from the oven and tray. If any excess honey seems to be still a little thin, simply boil it in the tray and reduce it to a thick, coating consistency. Pour over the duck and leave to rest for 15 minutes.

Remove the legs along with the breasts, making sure they are left whole. Sit the breast and leg for each portion on the plates, spooning over a tablespoon of honey and any residue. The slow-roast duck will be well done throughout; the meat will have become very tender and moist, just crumbling nicely as you eat it.

Note:
You may well find that after 2 hours the duck is completely roasted, tender and glazed.

I like simply to serve a good green salad, trickled with olive oil and a squeeze of lemon with this dish.

My Perfect Roast Chicken

Jamie Oliver

Serves 4

1.1-1.4kg (2½-3 lb) free-range chicken

salt and freshly ground black pepper

3 small handfuls of fresh herbs (basil, parsley, marjoram), picked and finely chopped

4 tablespoons olive oil

1 lemon, halved

4 bay leaves, torn

2 sprigs fresh rosemary

I cook this every week and I always try to do something different with it. Basically what I do is carefully part the skin from the meat on the top of the chicken breast and stuff the gap with fresh, delicate herbs such as parsley, basil and marjoram. Then I tie it up and roast it with some olive oil and salt.

Preheat the oven and a roasting tray to 225°C/425°F/Gas 7. Wash the chicken inside and out and pat it as dry as possible with kitchen paper. Some people remove the wishbone but I like to leave it in and make a wish. Rub the cavity with salt, then, being very careful, grab the skin at the tip of the chicken breasts, making sure that it doesn't rip, and pull up gently. With your other hand gently separate the skin from the meat of the breast. It's normally connected by a little bit of tissuey-type stuff, and you can either leave this attached in the middle and make two little tunnels either side or you can try to cut away the middle. Sprinkle a little salt down the gaps that you have made, and push in the chopped herbs. Drizzle in a little olive oil. I don't always stuff the chicken but when I do I generally go with lemon, bay and rosemary, which I push into the cavity at this point. Pull the skin of the chicken breast forward so that none of the actual flesh is exposed, tuck the little winglets under, and tie up as firmly as possible.

To me the perfect roast chicken has tender moist breast meat, crisp skin and, dare I say it, over-cooked thigh meat. So at this point, simply slash across each thigh about 3 or 4 times and rub in some of the leftover herbs, which allows the heat to penetrate directly into the thigh meat, enabling it to cook faster. With your hand, rub a little olive oil into the skin of the chicken and season very generously with salt and pepper. Remove the hot tray from the oven and add a little oil. Put the chicken, breast side down, on the bottom of the tray and put back into the oven. Allow to cook for 5 minutes, then turn it over on to the other side, breast side down. Cook for another 5 minutes and then place the chicken on its bottom. Cook for 1 hour at 220°C/425°F/Gas 7.

Use any excess fat that drips off into the roasting tray to roast your potatoes, or cook the potatoes in the tray with your chicken. The skin should be really crispy and the herbs will flavour the flesh - this really must be the best roast chicken. Trust me - it's not fiddly, it's pukka.

Left-over Chicken with a Mint, Chickpea and Lemon Salad

Serves 2

2 x 225g (8 oz) cooked chicken breasts	**James Martin**
1 x 250g (9 oz) tin chickpeas	
2 tablespoons chopped fresh mint	*A superb salad made*
juice and zest of 1 lemon	*with tinned chickpeas,*
1 tablespoon olive oil	*chicken and rocket.*
salt and freshly ground black pepper	
100g (3½ oz) rocket leaves	

Open the tin of chickpeas, drain off the liquid, then rinse the peas and drain again. Place in a bowl with the chopped mint, lemon juice and zest and olive oil. Season with salt and pepper.

Spoon the chickpeas on to a plate, leaving the dressing behind. Put the rocket leaves on the top and pour over the chickpea dressing.

Put the chicken on the top and serve. (If you have time, some diced cucumber and garlic mixed with yoghurt is a good garnish.)

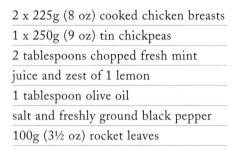

Hot Thai Stir-fry

Serves 2

a generous handful of basil leaves
(at least 20)

groundnut oil

350g (12 oz) chicken, cut into small
pieces but skin left on

4 spring onions, roughly chopped

small lump of ginger, about the size
of a walnut, peeled and shredded

3 garlic cloves, thinly sliced

2 hot red chillies, seeded and finely
chopped

2 tablespoons dark soy sauce

Nigel Slater

A quick, hot disguise for
inferior supermarket
chicken pieces. Made with
decent chicken the dish will
sing even louder. Some rice
might be a good idea as this
is not a substantial dish –
more of a light supper.

Tear the basil leaves up a bit. Heat a wok or deep frying pan and then pour in enough oil to cover the bottom, probably about 2 tablespoons. When the oil starts to shimmer and smoke, drop in the chopped chicken. If it lands skin-side down so much the better. Do not touch until the bottom side is golden, then move the chicken around in the pan. Chopsticks are as good as anything for this and will seem appropriate, though any old spoon is fine. Cook until the meat is golden on all sides. Test a piece; it should be juicy and only just cooked through. Tip out into a dish (anything will do, it is going back in the pan later).

Add a little more oil to the pan if there seems little left. Throw in the spring onions, ginger and garlic. Shake it all about a bit. It should sizzle and spit. If it doesn't then your pan isn't hot enough. Add the chillies. When they soften, return the chicken to the pan, throw in the basil and stir for a minute. Slosh in the soy sauce and serve on hot plates.

Corned-Beef Hash with Fried Eggs

Delia Smith

I love New York and, in particular, New York delis, where I always order a hot pastrami sandwich on rye bread and my husband always orders corned-beef hash with a fried egg. Although we don't have the same type of corned beef here, our humble, modest tinned version makes a mean old hash and, what's more, at an amazing price. A great meal made with incredible ease for under £1 a head!

Serves 2

7 oz (200g) tinned corned beef
2 large, very fresh eggs
2 tablespoons Worcestershire sauce
1 rounded teaspoon grain mustard
1 large onion
10 oz (275g) Desirée or King Edward potatoes
2-3 tablespoons groundnut or other flavourless oil
salt and freshly milled black pepper

You will also need a heavy-based frying pan approximately 8 inch (20cm) in diameter, a slightly smaller frying pan for the eggs and two plates placed in a warming oven.

Start this off by cutting the corned beef in half lengthways, then, using a sharp knife, cut each half into four ½ inch (1cm) pieces. Now chop these into ½ inch (1cm) dice, then scoop them all up into a bowl. Combine the Worcestershire sauce and mustard in a cup and pour this all over the beef, mixing it around to distribute it evenly.

Now peel and halve the onion, cut the halves into thin slices and then cut these in half. The potatoes need to be washed and cut into ½ inch (1cm) cubes, leaving the skin on, then place the cubes in a saucepan. Pour enough boiling water from the kettle to almost cover them, then add salt and a lid and simmer for just 5 minutes before draining them in a colander and then covering with a clean tea cloth to absorb the steam.

Now heat 2 tablespoons of the oil in the frying pan and, when it's smoking hot, add the sliced onions and toss them around in the oil to brown for about 3 minutes altogether, keeping the heat high, as they need to be very well browned at the edges.

After that, push all the onions to the edge of the pan and, still keeping the heat very high, add the potatoes and toss these around, too, because they also need to be quite brown. Add a little more oil here if necessary. Now add some seasoning, then, using a pan slice, keep turning the potatoes and onions over to hit the heat. After about 6 minutes, add the beef and continue to toss everything around to allow the beef to heat through (about 3 minutes).

After that, turn the heat down to its lowest setting and, in the smaller frying pan, fry the eggs. (Place the pan over a high heat and, as soon as 1 dessertspoon of fat or oil is really hot, carefully break the eggs in. After 30 seconds turn the heat down to medium and carry on cooking them, tilting the pan and basting the eggs with the hot fat so that the tops can be lightly cooked, too. After about 1 minute remove the pan from the heat, then lift the eggs out with a kitchen slice. Let them rest on some kitchen paper for a couple of seconds.) Serve the hash divided between the two warm plates with an egg on top of each and don't forget to have plenty of tomato ketchup on the table.

Note: There's now a tomato ketchup available in wholefood shops that does not contain sugar and has a real tomato flavour.

Braised Ham with Mustard Sauce

Serves 10

2.7kg (6 lb) piece of gammon/bacon joint

½ bottle medium dry white wine

handful cloves

2 tablespoons peppercorns

½ bottle Madeira

Brian Turner

For the sauce

8 shallots

300ml (½ pint) dry white wine

300ml (½ pint) vegetable/ham stock

75g (3 oz) butter

40g (1½ oz) plain flour

1 tablespoon juniper berries

1 tablespoon green peppercorns in brine

120ml (4 fl oz) white wine vinegar

2 tablespoons Dijon mustard

120ml (4 fl oz) crème fraîche

salt and freshly ground black pepper

Soak gammon overnight in cold water. Drain and dry well.

Calculate cooking time – allow 25 minutes per 450g (1 lb).

Place gammon in large pan, cover with cold water and bring to the boil, then drain off the water.

Add the wine to pan, add cloves and peppercorns and enough hot water to cover.

Cover and simmer according to weight of gammon. Cool in liquid. Drain.

Preheat oven to 180°C/350°F/Gas 4.

Remove rind from gammon and score fat into diamond pattern. Place gammon in roasting tin and pour over the Madeira.

Braise in oven for 1 hour approx., basting frequently. Remove gammon.

Chop shallots.

Pour juices from roasting tin into a bowl and skim off any fat. Make up the braising liquid to 900ml (1½ pints) with wine and stock. Melt the butter in a pan. Stir in the flour and then add the stock and wine mixture.

Sprinkle in the juniper berries and half the shallots. Simmer for 10 minutes.

Place the rest of the shallots, green peppercorns and vinegar in a pan. Reduce to 2 teaspoons.

Cool the pan and stir the Madeira sauce into the reduced vinegar.

Add the mustard and simmer again for 10 minutes. Stir in the crème fraîche.

Serve ham with the sauce and seasonal vegetables or a salad.

Pork Meatballs with Coriander Couscous

Serves 4

For the couscous

115g (4 oz) couscous	
350ml (12 fl oz) vegetable stock, hot	
50ml (2 fl oz) olive oil	
bunch of fresh coriander, chopped	
3 red and 3 green chillies, deseeded and finely chopped	
2 teaspoons chilli oil	

For the meatballs

175g (6 oz) onion, finely chopped
2 cloves garlic, crushed
450g (1 lb) minced lean pork
2 egg yolks
1 teaspoon cinnamon
2 teaspoons chilli powder
2 teaspoons paprika
1 teaspoon cumin seeds
vegetable oil, for frying
salt and freshly ground black pepper

For the sauce

50ml (2 fl oz) olive oil
115g (4 oz) onion, finely chopped
3 cloves garlic, crushed
675g (1½ lb) over-ripe tomatoes, peeled, deseeded and chopped
2 tablespoons sun-dried tomato purée
2 glasses dry white wine
½ teaspoon Tabasco sauce
½ teaspoon Worcestershire sauce
pinch of caster sugar

Kevin Woodford

The inspiration for this dish came from the Indian and Pakistan communities in Yorkshire.

MAIN COURSES

34

To make the couscous, place the couscous in a bowl and pour the vegetable stock over it, season with salt and mix in the olive oil. Allow to stand for 10 minutes and then add the chopped coriander, red and green chillies and chilli oil and cover with clear film.

To make the meatballs, mix together the onion, garlic and minced pork. Add the egg yolks, cinnamon, chilli powder and paprika. Crush the cumin seeds in the palm of your hand prior to sprinkling them into the mixture and season with salt and pepper. Divide the mixture into 20 small meatballs and gently cook in a frying pan containing hot oil, turning frequently.

To prepare the sauce, heat the olive oil and cook the onion and garlic, add the chopped tomatoes and cook for 3-4 minutes. Add the sun-dried tomato purée, white wine, Tabasco and Worcestershire sauce, season with salt, pepper and a pinch of caster sugar.

To serve, microwave the couscous on high for 45 seconds, spoon into tightly buttered ramekins or dariole moulds and unmould onto the centre of a serving plate. Surround the couscous with 5 meatballs and top each one with tomato sauce.

Spicy Shepherd's Pie with Spinach and Sesame Seeds

Serves 6

675g (1½ lb) large floury potatoes, chopped	**Josceline Dimbleby**
1 tablespoon fromage frais	
3 tablespoons olive oil, plus extra	*The secret of a good*
2 medium onions, preferably red, finely chopped	*minced meat dish is to*
2 teaspoons ground cumin	*add lots of flavour, and*
2 teaspoons ground cinnamon	*spices are ideal for this.*
750g (1¾ lb) lean minced lamb	*This pie is made with*
2 tablespoons tomato purée	*minced lamb – as*
generous handful fresh mint, finely chopped	*shepherd's pie should be*
225g (8 oz) fresh spinach, finely chopped	*– and has slightly*
2 eggs, lightly whisked	*Middle Eastern hints.*
2 tablespoons sesame seeds	
salt and freshly ground black pepper	

Preheat the oven to 180°C/350°F/Gas 4. Steam or boil the potatoes, then mash them, mixing in the fromage frais. Leave to cool.

Heat the oil in a large, heavy frying pan. Add the onions, stir until just softened, then transfer from the pan to a large bowl.

Turn up the heat and add the spices and lamb to the pan; stir constantly, breaking up the lamb, for 8-10 minutes until the juices evaporate. Stir in the tomato purée, remove from the heat and add to the onions.

Stir the mint into the lamb mixture and season well. Spoon the mixture into a shallow, ovenproof dish and arrange the spinach evenly on top.

Stir the eggs into the cooled potato and season, then spoon it over the spinach. Sprinkle with sesame seeds and drizzle with a little oil. Bake for 1½ hours until rich, golden brown.

Beef Stew with Red Wine and Brandy

Serves 10-12

1.75g (4 lb) piece silverside or top rump pork or goose fat
2 large onions, sliced
5 largish carrots, halved lengthways
2 plump cloves garlic, slightly crushed
120ml (4 fl oz) brandy
½ bottle of the Bulgarian Melnik
450g (1 lb) streaky salt pork, cut into cubes
2 pigs' trotters (split)
2 bay leaves, thyme and parsley
salt and freshly ground black pepper

Jennifer Paterson

Topside of beef seems to be usually recommended for stewing but I think the unsalted silverside is more the thing, or, more expensively, top rump. I have cooked this dish with the Bulgarian Reserve Melnik 1983 which I find very good both for the pot and the table.

Have the meat tied into a neat shape for the heavy casserole you will be using. Melt about 50g (2 oz) of the fat in the pot, place the meat in the middle and surround it with the onions, carrots and garlic cloves. Cook gently for 15 minutes until the onions have taken on a little colour and you have browned the meat all over.

Pour in the brandy, let it bubble, then add the wine, the salt pork and the pigs' trotters, which will enrich the sauce. Tuck the herbs into the dish, season with a little salt and freshly ground pepper. Cover with foil and a well-fitting lid. Place in the lowest possible oven for about 7 hours.

This will produce a delicious and tender piece of meat with a rather fatty sauce, so serve some plain boiled potatoes with it. If it is served cold, remove the vegetables immediately, and the fat when the jelly has set.

Glazed Lamb Shanks

Serves 4

4 lamb shanks, weighing 350g (12 oz) each

sea salt and freshly ground black pepper

4 tablespoons olive oil

8 medium shallots, peeled

4 small turnips, peeled

2 medium carrots, peeled and halved

Raymond Blanc

The entire dish may be made in advance and then gently reheated.

Season the lamb shanks then sear them in the oil in a large pan for 6-8 minutes until golden brown. Drain off all the fat then add the vegetables and cover with water. Bring to the boil, skim off all the impurities and as much of the fat as possible, then cook at just below simmering point for 2½ hours. Make sure they remain covered with liquid. Very gently, as the shanks will be extremely delicate, transfer them and the vegetables to an oven dish or tray with a slotted spoon.

Preheat the oven to 200°C/400°F/Gas 6.

Skim the fat off the top of the stock and boil to reduce by two-thirds, skimming frequently. Pour the stock over the top of the shanks and vegetables, then place in the oven for 20 minutes, basting regularly until they have a shining glaze. Serve with sea salt and freshly ground black pepper.

Note:
The shanks must be cooked very slowly, at below simmering point, so that they remain moist and tender; cooked at too high a temperature, they will toughen and become stringy.

Noodles with Spring Onions, Shitake Mushrooms and Mangetouts ♈

Serves 4

Nigella Lawson

250g (9 oz) egg noodles	
2 tablespoons vegetable oil	
1 teaspoon sesame oil	
4 red chillies, deseeded and chopped	
6 spring onions, chopped into 1cm lengths	
240g (8½ oz) mushrooms, destalked and chopped	
100g (3½ oz) mangetouts, roughly chopped (in half or 3 pieces each)	
2 tablespoons soy sauce	
fresh chopped coriander	

Just as you can boil the noodles in good time, so you can chop all the bits to go in them. I know stir-frying can tax a girl's nerves, but this is serenely manageable.

Boil the noodles in salted water according to the instructions on the packet, then drain, rinse in cold water and drain again.

Heat the oils in a hot wok or large frying pan and stir-fry the chilli and spring onion for one minute, add the shitake mushrooms and stir-fry for another two minutes. Then add, stirring furiously, the mangetouts. Give them a minute, then add the noodles, lifting them up in the pan and stirring well so all is mixed in together, pouring in a couple of tablespoons soy as you do so.

Toss well and quickly, then empty into a big round plate. Sprinkle with coriander.

Pine Nut, Spinach and Two Cheese Pasta Salad ♈

Serves 4

250g (9oz) small pasta bows (farfalle)	
100g (4 oz) small broccoli florets	
100g (4 oz) baby spinach leaves	
1 tablespoon sunflower oil	
4 tablespoons basil oil	
2 tablespoons red wine vinegar	
1 small garlic clove, crushed	
95g (3 oz) toasted pine nuts	
very generous handful of fresh basil (shredded)	
50g (2 oz) Parmesan, coarsely grated	
100g (4 oz) soft goat's cheese, crumbled	

Orlando Murrin

This very fresh, light salad has all the flavour of pesto without the oiliness. And with two cheeses, a fragrant herb dressing and lots of greenery, it's a hearty meal.

Cook the pasta in a pan of boiling salted water according to the packet instructions, adding the broccoli for the last 3-4 minutes of cooking time; drain well and return to the pan. Stir in the spinach while the pasta is still hot so it just wilts; set aside.

Mix together the two oils, vinegar and garlic, and season with salt and pepper. Toss the pasta and vegetables with the dressing, toasted pine nuts, basil and two cheeses.

Sinhalese Pasta Prawns with Lemon

Serves 4

6 tablespoons olive oil

450g (1 lb) fresh or dried linguine

½ small onion, finely chopped

1 garlic clove, crushed

1 tablespoon mild curry powder

225g (8 oz) cooked peeled prawns

1 tablespoon each chopped fresh coriander, mint and parsley

juice and grated rind of 1 lemon

salt and freshly ground black pepper

handful of mixed fresh herb sprigs, to garnish

Ainsley Harriott

If linguine is not available, use spaghetti instead. Verna (Berna) lemons (if you can find them) are ideal in this recipe – they're on sale from March to August.

Bring a large pan of salted water to the boil and add a drop of the olive oil. Add the linguine and cook according to the instructions on the packet; drain.

Heat the remaining oil in a large frying pan or wok and fry the onion and garlic until the onion is softened but not coloured. Add the curry powder and fry for 20 seconds, stirring continuously. Add the prawns, chopped herbs and lemon rind.

Toss together to heat through, then sprinkle over the lemon juice and season. Garnish with herb sprigs and serve at once.

Penne alla Vodka con Caviale

**Serves 2 as a main course,
4 as a starter**

225g (8 oz) penne

4 tablespoons passata or peeled,
deseeded and liquidized fresh tomatoes

6 tablespoons double cream

1 tablespoon vodka

salt and freshly ground black pepper

To garnish

2-4 teaspoons caviar, preferably Sevruga

2 teaspoons chopped fresh chives

Sophie Grigson

*Back in the late seventies
and early eighties, this
pasta dish enjoyed a brief
fashionable status. I first
ate it in Rome, in a student
flat, and adored it instantly.
Whenever I can afford the
caviar I turn back to it
with renewed enthusiasm,
even if it isn't considered
modern or stylish any more.*

Bring a large pan of lightly salted water to the boil and tip in the penne. Cook according to packet instructions until *al dente*. Drain well and transfer to a warm serving dish.

While the pasta cooks, place the passata or liquidized fresh tomatoes and cream in a small pan. Simmer for 5 minutes to thicken slightly, stirring occasionally. Draw off the heat, let the bubbles subside, then stir in the vodka and season.

When the pasta is ready, bring the tomato mixture back to the boil and pour it over the pasta. Spoon the caviar on top and sprinkle with the chives. Toss at the table and serve.

Conchiglie with Ricotta and Rocket ♈

Serves 6

1kg (2¼ lb) rocket leaves	
100ml (3½ fl oz) extra virgin olive oil	
3 garlic cloves, peeled and roughly chopped	
4 tablespoons fresh basil leaves, torn into pieces	
2 fresh red chillies, seeded and chopped	
Maldon salt and freshly ground black pepper	
400g (14 oz) conchiglie	
200g (7 oz) ricotta, lightly beaten with a fork	
150g (5 oz) Parmesan, freshly grated	

Ruth Rogers and Rose Gray

A subtle southern Italian sauce combining delicate fresh ricotta with fiery red chillies.

Wash the rocket and dry in a salad spinner. Divide the quantity into two, and roughly chop one half.

Heat a large, thick-bottomed saucepan and add 2 tablespoons of the oil. Gently fry the garlic until it begins to turn gold, then add the torn-up basil leaves and the whole rocket leaves. Put on the lid and let the rocket wilt – this takes 2-3 minutes. Put the hot wilted rocket and any liquid in the pan into a food processor and pulse-chop. Add half of the chopped rocket and blend again to combine. Stir in the chilli, salt, pepper and the remaining olive oil.

Cook the pasta in a generous amount of boiling salted water. Drain, return to the pan, and add the rocket sauce. Turn the pasta over gently to coat each shell. Finally, lightly fork in the ricotta and the remaining chopped rocket. Season, and serve with the Parmesan.

Farfalle with Mint, Prosciutto and Peas

Serves 6

2kg (4½ lb) young fresh peas in their pods or 150g (5 oz) frozen petits pois
50g (2 oz) unsalted butter
1 medium red onion or sweet white onion, peeled and chopped
1 bunch fresh mint, stalks removed, roughly chopped
10 slices prosciutto di Parma
150ml (¼ pint) double cream
Maldon salt and freshly ground black pepper
500g (18 oz) farfalle
100g (4 oz) Parmesan, freshly grated

Ruth Rogers and Rose Gray

Using a thick-bottomed saucepan, gently heat the butter. Add the onion and fry gently until soft and beginning to colour. Add the peas and one-third of the mint and stir to combine. Pour over enough water to just cover the peas, then carefully place 4 slices of prosciutto on the top. Simmer very gently for 5-10 minutes, or until the peas are soft, adding more water if the level goes below that of the peas.

Put half the sauce into a blender, including the prosciutto. Add half of the remaining mint and pulse-chop to a rough texture. Return to the pan and stir to combine the two different textured sauces. Add the cream, the remaining mint, salt and pepper and bring to the boil. Remove from the heat and add the remaining peas.

Cook the farfalle in a generous amount of boiling salted water, drain and add to the sauce.

Tear the remaining prosciutto into smaller pieces and add to the pasta mixture. Serve with the Parmesan.

Sautéed Red Mullet with Parsley, Garlic and Spaghettini

Serves 4

4 small red mullet, weighing about 150g (5 oz) each, filleted	**Rick Stein**
450g (1 lb) spaghettini	*I always think that*
4 tablespoons olive oil	*a good pile of pasta*
2 garlic cloves, finely chopped	*is what everybody*
1 red finger chilli, seeded and finely chopped	
4 plum tomatoes, skinned, seeded and chopped	*really likes. This*
20g (¾ oz) flatleaf parsley, finely chopped	*one is the business*
salt and freshly ground black pepper	*and so easy.*
extra virgin olive oil to serve	

Cut the red mullet fillets across into strips 2cm (¾ in) wide.

Bring 3.4 litres (6 pints) of water to the boil in a large pan with
2 tablespoons of salt. Add the pasta, bring back to the boil and boil for
5 minutes or until *al dente*.

Meanwhile heat the olive oil in a large frying pan. Fry the strips of red
mullet, skin-side down, for 3 minutes. Turn them over, fry for
1 minute and then season with salt and pepper.

Drain the pasta well and tip it into a large serving bowl. Add the garlic
and red chilli to the frying pan with the red mullet and fry for 30
seconds. Add the tomatoes and fry for a further 30 seconds. Tip
everything into the bowl with the pasta, scraping up all the little bits
that may have stuck to the bottom of the pan, then add
3 tablespoons of the parsley and gently toss everything together so that
the fish just begins to break up.

Serve immediately, drizzled with extra virgin olive oil and sprinkled
with the remaining chopped parsley.

Hake in Serrano Ham with Capers and Saffron Pasta

Ross Burden

Serves 6

6 pieces of hake fillet, cut from the thick part, each about 150g (5½ oz)

6 slices of Serrano or Parma ham

4 tablespoons plain flour

6 tablespoons olive oil

6 sprigs of fresh chervil to garnish

For the pasta

300g (10½ oz) dried taglialini or similar thin noodles

juice of ½ lemon

pinch of saffron threads

150g (5½ oz) chilled butter, cut into pieces

For the sauce

280g (10 oz) shelled fresh peas or frozen petits pois

225g (8 oz) frozen broad beans, thawed and skinned

2 tablespoons good capers, rinsed and drained

2 tablespoons chopped parsley

juice of ½ lemon

Hake, a delicious, flaky white fish, is vastly underrated in this country, but is consumed in enormous amounts in the Iberian peninsula. If you can't find hake, this method also works well with cod and haddock.

The fish should be with its skin but scaled, as the skin is such a pretty silver and will show through the cooked ham. Wrap each piece in a slice of ham, then dredge with flour. Heat a little of the olive oil and add the fish, serving side down. Fry for 2-3 minutes or until browned and crispy, then turn and fry the other side until just cooked. Remove and keep warm in a low oven. Set the pan aside.

Cook the pasta in boiling salted water until *al dente*.

Meanwhile, for the sauce, blanch fresh peas in boiling water for

1 minute, then drain. Frozen petits pois only need to be thawed. Set aside.

Heat the lemon juice in a saucepan with the same quantity of water and the saffron. Beat in the chilled butter. Keep warm to maintain the emulsion. When the pasta is cooked, drain well and dress in the butter sauce. Using a long-pronged carving fork, form skeins in much the same way as one eats spaghetti and pile on one side of individual plates or on to a large serving platter. Keep hot.

Drain off most of the oil from the fish pan, then add the peas, beans, capers and parsley to the pan and gently warm through. (Too much heat will change the colour of the ingredients.) Add the rest of the oil and the lemon juice, season and mix well.

Place each piece of fish on a pile of the vegetables next to the saffron pasta and use the warmed oil mixture as a sauce. Garnish with chervil and serve.

Risotto of Greens, Garlic, Anchovies and Capers

Serves 4

2 tablespoons extra virgin olive oil	
1 onion, finely chopped	
3 cloves garlic, finely chopped	
5 anchovy fillets, drained and chopped	
350g (12 oz) arborio rice	
2 litres (3½ pints) chicken or vegetable stock, boiling	
8 handfuls salad leaves (rocket, spinach, escarole, mustard greens), ripped	
55g (2 oz) unsalted butter	
115g (4 oz) Parmesan, freshly grated	
freshly ground black pepper	
2 tablespoons tiny capers, drained and rinsed	

Antony Worrall Thompson

A delicious risotto

making full use of

different salad leaves.

One advantage of wilting

leaves is that you don't

have to be too fussy about

the quality of the leaf –

outsize, outside and

secondary leaves are

all fair game.

In a large saucepan heat the olive oil, add the onion and garlic, and cook over a medium heat until the onion has softened without colour, about 8-10 minutes.

Add the anchovies and rice and stir to coat the grains in the oil. Cook for 2 minutes until the rice becomes translucent.

Add a ladle or two of stock. Stir the rice until it has absorbed most of the stock. Add a little more stock and repeat. Continue to add stock little by little until the rice is almost cooked. The mixture should be creamy without being too wet.

Add the greens and cook for a further 3 minutes until the leaves have wilted. Fold in the butter and Parmesan and stir to combine. Season to taste with pepper.

Just before serving fold in the capers. Remember that risotto continues to cook after you remove it from the heat, so serve immediately.

Lemon Sole with Grapes and White Wine Sauce

Phil Vickery

Serves 4

4 lemon sole fillets (free of skin and bone)

1 glass white wine

salt and freshly ground black pepper

sugar

150ml (¼ pint) well-flavoured fish stock

300ml (½ pint) double cream

lemon juice

small bunch of sorrel

24 green seedless grapes, cut in half

900g (2 lb) spinach, cooked, refreshed and squeezed out

a little butter and nutmeg

This is one of my

all-time favourites.

It both looks and

tastes delicious.

Place the white wine and a pinch of salt and sugar in a small pan and bring to the boil.

Once the wine is boiling, add the fish stock and reduce by two-thirds, until syrupy. Add the double cream and bring back to the boil. Season with salt, pepper and lemon juice and reserve.

Fold under both ends of the fillets, place them on buttered foil and season with salt and pepper.

Place the fillets in a gently boiling steamer and steam for 3-4 minutes.

Meanwhile, trim and wash the sorrel. Bring the sauce back to the boil, add the sorrel and reduce the heat. Add the grapes.

Warm the spinach in a little butter and season with salt, pepper and nutmeg.

To serve, place each sole fillet on top of some spinach, and spoon the grape and sorrel sauce over the fish.

Grilled Swordfish with Green Lentil Salad

Serves 2

400g (14 oz) can green lentils

2 plum tomatoes, peeled, seeded and finely diced

50g (2 oz) red or green peppers (or a mixture), seeded and finely diced

1 red or green chilli, seeded and finely chopped

1 spring onion, finely chopped

2 tablespoons soy sauce

1 tablespoon white wine vinegar

3 tablespoons olive oil

1 tablespoon chopped fresh herbs, such as coriander, basil and parsley

salt and freshly ground black pepper

2 x 175g (6 oz) swordfish steaks

fresh coriander sprigs, to garnish

Ainsley Harriott

Swordfish is a firm, succulent fish that has become popular over the past few years. The lentil salad complements it nicely.

Place the lentils in a pan and warm slightly; remove from heat and drain. Transfer to a large bowl, then add the tomatoes, peppers, chilli and spring onion; mix well. Mix the soy sauce, vinegar, 2 tablespoons of olive oil, herbs and seasoning into the lentil mixture. Mix together well and set aside.

Heat a large ridged grill pan until hot. Season the swordfish steaks and brush with the remaining olive oil. Grill for 2-3 minutes on each side, depending on the thickness of the fish. Place a mound of lentil salad on each of four serving plates, set the swordfish steaks on top, then garnish with the coriander sprigs and serve.

La Mouclade

Serves 4

Rick Stein

a good pinch of saffron
1.75kg (4 lb) mussels, cleaned
120ml (4 fl oz) dry white wine
25g (1 oz) butter
1 small onion, finely chopped
2 garlic cloves, finely chopped
½ teaspoon good-quality medium curry powder
2 tablespoons cognac
2 teaspoons plain flour
200ml (7 fl oz) crème fraîche
3 tablespoons chopped parsley
salt and freshly ground black pepper

This brilliantly creamy, rich dish is full of delicate traces of saffron and spice and is a testimony to the ability of the French to take a foreign flavour and make it seeem as though it has been French forever.

Put the saffron into a small bowl and moisten it with 1 tablespoon of warm water. Place the mussels and the wine in a large pan, cover and cook over a high heat for 3-4 minutes, shaking the pan now and then, until the mussels have opened. Tip them into a colander set over a bowl to catch all the cooking liquor, and discard any that haven't opened. Transfer the mussels to a large serving bowl and keep warm.

Melt the butter in a pan, add the onion, garlic and curry powder and cook gently without browning for 2-3 minutes. Add the cognac and cook until it has almost evaporated, then stir in the flour and cook for 1 minute. Gradually stir in the saffron liquid and all but the last tablespoon or two of the mussel cooking liquor, which might contain some grit. Bring the sauce to a simmer and cook for 2-3 minutes. Add the cream and simmer for a further 3 minutes, until slightly reduced.

Season to taste, stir in the parsley and then pour the sauce over the mussels. Stir them together gently and serve with plenty of French bread.

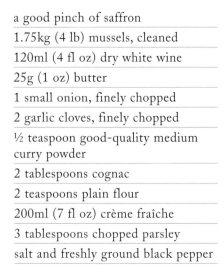

Salmon en Croûte with Lemon Cream Sauce

Serves 6-8

350g (12 oz) white fish, such as haddock, whiting or cod
175g (6 oz) fresh white breadcrumbs
juice and grated rind of 1 lemon
1 tablespoon snipped fresh chives
1 tablespoon chopped fresh parsley
1 egg
4 tablespoons sunflower oil
450g (1 lb) ready-made puff pastry, thawed if frozen
2 large salmon fillets
1 egg, beaten, to glaze
salt and freshly ground black pepper

Michael Barry

Ask your fishmonger

to fillet a 1.25kg

(2½ lb) salmon and

keep the bones and

trimmings for the

lemon cream sauce

(see opposite).

Preheat the oven to 200°C/400°F/Gas 6. Put the white fish, breadcrumbs, lemon juice and rind, chives, parsley, egg and oil in a food processor. Whizz until smooth, then season to taste.

Roll out the pastry to a long, oval shape 15cm (6 inches) longer than a salmon fillet and 2½ times as wide. Place a fillet in the centre of the pastry, spread over the white fish paste and sandwich with the other fillet.

Cut diagonal lines along each side of the puff pastry about 1cm (½ inch) apart, leaving 7.5cm (3 inches) at each end uncut. Bring together the sides of the pastry, criss-cross the cut strips over each other and secure them with beaten egg. Fold one end of the pastry into a triangle to make the shape of a fish head and cut a wedge from the other end to make the shape of a tail.

Lift fish on to a greased baking tray. Brush pastry with beaten egg and bake for 35-40 minutes. The fish is ready when a skewer inserted between the plaits comes out clean. Serve on its own or with lemon cream sauce.

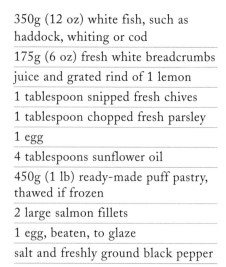

Lemon Cream Sauce

Makes about 150ml (¼ pint)

fish trimmings and bones
juice of ½ lemon
1 bay leaf
4 peppercorns
4 tablespoons double cream
salt and freshly ground black pepper

Boil the fish trimmings and bones, lemon juice, bay leaf and peppercorns in a little water for 10 minutes.

Strain the liquid into a clean pan, then boil rapidly until it has reduced to about 150ml (¼ pint).

Stir in the cream and season to taste.

Sardines Beccafico-style

Serves 4

200g (7 oz) fresh white breadcrumbs

juice of 3 oranges

juice of 2 lemons

3 tablespoons olive oil

4 tablespoons pine nuts

4 tablespoons raisins

pinch of sugar

12 fresh sardines, cleaned, boned
and opened flat

handful fresh bay leaves

salt and freshly ground black pepper

Antonio Carluccio

I love the clean citrus

flavours of this

Sicilian dish.

Preheat the oven to 200°C/400°F/Gas 6. Place the breadcrumbs in a pan and dry fry until golden, then mix with the juice from two of the oranges and half of the lemon juice. Stir in 1 tablespoon of the oil, the pine nuts, raisins, sugar and seasoning.

Put a spoonful of breadcrumb paste in the centre of each of the sardines and roll up tightly. Arrange in an ovenproof dish with a bay leaf tucked between each fish. Drizzle over remaining oil and bake for 15 minutes, then drizzle over the remaining citrus juices. Serve immediately.

MAIN COURSES

Grilled Mackerel with a Sweet Chilli Glaze on Mixed Bean Salad

Serves 6

Peter Gordon

6 large boneless mackerel fillets

A fresh spin on preparing mackerel, using exotic flavours and different textures.

For the bean salad
a selection of mangetout, green beans, broad beans and sugar snaps

20ml (4 teaspoons) lemon juice

2 pinches sea salt

60ml (4 tablespoons) extra virgin olive oil

For the sweet chilli glaze
1 teaspoon dried chilli flakes

½ cup light brown sugar

2 teaspoons light soy sauce

4 teaspoons lemon juice

¼ teaspoon finely ground allspice

Prepare the bean salad by lightly blanching the beans in separate batches until they are just cooked but still have a crunch. Refresh them under cold water and dress with a little lemon juice, sea salt and extra virgin olive oil.

Put all the ingredients for the sweet chilli glaze into a small pan, bring to the boil, and cook until the mix starts to thicken and remove from the heat.

Place the mackerel fillets, skin side up, on an oiled piece of foil under a hot grill for 2 minutes, then turn over and grill for another minute. Cooking times will vary with the thickness of the fillet - aim to keep the fish pink in the middle. Brush with the glaze and return to the grill until the glaze just begins to 'burn'. Remove the mackerel from the tray and serve on top of the beans.

Parmesan-crusted Salmon with a Mussel and Coriander Chowder

Serves 4

4 x 175g (6 oz) salmon fillets, skinned and boned

salt and freshly ground black pepper

small bunch fresh coriander

1 tablespoon olive oil

25g (1 oz) Parmesan, freshly grated

For the mussel chowder

1kg (2 lb) mussels, cleaned

1 tablespoon olive oil

1 rasher smoked bacon, rinded and chopped

1 onion, peeled and finely chopped

1 clove garlic, peeled and finely chopped

200ml (7 fl oz) dry white wine

1 carrot, peeled and finely diced

1 leek, trimmed, finely diced and washed

1 potato, peeled and finely diced

200ml (7 fl oz) whipping cream

1 tablespoon chopped fresh coriander

Andrew Nutter

My dream fish dish: perfectly moist salmon topped with melting Parmesan, served on a pool of creamy bacon and mussel sauce. Follow this recipe and you won't just be dreaming – you'll be in heaven.

Preheat the oven to 150°C/300°F/Gas 2/fan oven 130°C.

Make a horizontal cut half-way into each salmon fillet. Lift the top flap, season under it with salt and pepper, lay on a few leaves of coriander and re-form the fillet.

Heat a frying pan and put in the olive oil. Seal the salmon on both sides until it is golden brown. Sprinkle the fish with Parmesan, put it on a baking sheet and bake in the oven for about 10 minutes, or until the fish is cooked through.

Meanwhile, make the mussel chowder. Heat the olive oil in a saucepan. Add the bacon and fry until it is golden brown. Then put in the onion and garlic and cook, until slightly softened, for 3-4 minutes. Add the mussels - discard any open ones - to the saucepan, pour in the white wine, cover, and leave to cook for 2-3 minutes, shaking the pan occasionally until the mussels have opened. Remove them with a slotted spoon, discarding any that are still closed. Keep them warm.

Add the carrot, leek and potato to the white wine and mussel juices in the saucepan and cook until the vegetables are tender, for 10-12 minutes.

Now pour in the cream and bring to the boil. Add the chopped coriander, then return the mussels to the pan and warm through until they are sufficiently hot to serve. Over-cooking the mussels at this stage, though, will toughen them.

Serve the chunky mussel chowder around the Parmesan-crusted salmon in large soup bowls. It's orgasmic!

Red Mullet with Green Olive Tapenade and Courgettes

Serves 4

Raymond Blanc

8 x 70g (3oz) very fresh fillets of
red mullet, skin on

salt and freshly ground black pepper

4 tablespoons olive oil

3 medium courgettes, cut into
4mm (¼ inch) thick slices

1 large bunch of rocket, leaves
picked and chopped

2 garlic cloves, peeled and chopped

2 tablespoons capers, well rinsed

1 recipe *Tapenade* made with green
olives (see below)

½ bunch of fresh flatleaf parsley,
leaves picked and finely chopped

For the *Tapenade*

100g (4 oz) stoned black olives

2 garlic cloves, peeled

50ml (2 fl oz) extra virgin olive oil

Heat two frying pans. Spoon 2 tablespoons of the olive oil into each of
them. Into one, toss the courgettes, and into the other place the
seasoned red mullet fillets, skin side down. Fry the red mullet for
2 minutes, then turn and fry for 30 seconds on the flesh side. Turn off
the heat and allow to rest while you finish the courgettes.

Once the courgettes have been sautéed for 2 minutes, add the rocket,
garlic and capers. Toss until the rocket has softened, then season to taste.

To make the *tapenade* purée the ingredients together in a food
processor. You will not need to season it.

Mix the *tapenade* with the parsley and spread on half the mullet fillets.
Serve one 'red' fillet and one 'green' fillet per person on top of the
courgette and rocket mixture.

Scallops Cha Cha Cha

Serves 2

small bunch of wild
(or cultivated) chives

small bunch of wild chervil
(or parsley)

½ teaspoon finely chopped
fresh red chilli

a little olive oil

6 large scallops, cleaned,
without corals

Hugh Fearnley-Whittingstall

I invented the rather silly

name for this lovely dish

on account of the

three flavourings in the

dressing: chives, chervil

and chillies. It is

extremely simple,

but exquisite.

Heat a cast-iron skillet, or heavy frying pan, without any oil until very hot.

Chop the chives and chervil and mix with the chopped chillies and a little olive oil, to get a green and red flecked dressing.

Lightly brush both sides of each scallop with olive oil, and place quickly on the hot pan. Leave for exactly 1 minute, then carefully turn them over. Cook for another minute, then remove.

Place 3 scallops each on 2 warmed plates, and trickle them with the cha-cha-cha dressing. Eat at once.

Salmon Fish Cakes with Quick Tartare Sauce

Serves 4

3 spring onions, finely chopped, including some of the green tops

120ml (4 fl oz) white wine

225g (8 oz) tinned red salmon

225g (8 oz) mashed potatoes

grated zest of lemon

a dash of anchovy essence

salt and freshly ground black pepper

some finely chopped parsley

plain flour for coating

1 beaten egg

75g (3 oz) fresh brown breadcrumbs

oil for frying

a knob of butter

Jane Asher

These delicious fish cakes are just the thing for an easy family supper.

Soften the onion in the wine, drain and cool. Remove skin and bones from the salmon, drain and flake and mix with the potatoes. Add lemon zest, anchovy essence, salt and pepper, the cooled onions and chopped parsley to taste. With floured hands, shape into four cakes, dip into beaten egg, then breadcrumbs.

Chill in the fridge before cooking in a frying pan with oil and a knob of butter on medium heat for approximately 3 minutes each side until golden.

Quick Tartare Sauce

150ml (¼ pint) mayonnaise

1 dessertspoon finely chopped onion

1 tablespoon chopped capers or gherkins

1 teaspoon lemon juice

Mix together and serve with the fish cakes.

Vegetable and Cheese Pâté

Serves 4-6

12 small young carrots

12 haricots verts or French beans

salt and freshly ground black pepper

225ml (7½ fl oz) milk

1 medium onion, finely chopped

1 garlic clove, chopped

25g (1 oz) butter or margarine

25g (1 oz) plain flour

3 tablespoons dry white wine

11g (0.4 oz) (1 sachet) gelatine

350g (12 oz) mature Cheddar cheese, finely grated

1 teaspoon Dijon mustard

1 tablespoon finely chopped parsley

2 teaspoons finely chopped chives

3 tablespoons sun-dried tomatoes, finely chopped

145ml (scant ¼ pint) double cream

To garnish

lemon slices

mixed salad

Marguerite Patten

This can be served as a light main dish. When sliced it is full of colour from the vegetables.

Scrape the carrots and string the beans. Put into a little well-seasoned boiling water and cook until just tender. Strain and dry well on absorbent paper.

Put the milk, onion and garlic into a saucepan, simmer for 5 minutes then strain. You should have just 150ml (¼ pint) – if less add extra to make this quantity. Heat the butter or margarine in the saucepan, stir in the flour then the strained milk and continue to stir over a low heat until a thick sauce, keep this hot.

Pour the wine into a basin, add the gelatine, allow to stand for 3 minutes then dissolve over hot water or in a microwave. Stir into the hot sauce until well blended. Add the cheese, mustard, herbs, sun-dried tomatoes and seasoning; allow to cool. Whip the cream and fold into the cheese mixture.

Lightly oil a 900g (2 lb) loaf tin or mould. Spoon in one third of the cheese mixture. Arrange half the carrots and beans over this. Cover with half the cheese mixture, then the remaining vegetables and finally with the rest of the cheese mixture. Leave in the refrigerator until firm. Turn out and garnish with lemon slices and salad.

Variation:
Use mascarpone cheese instead of double cream.

Michelle's Mélange ♈

Patrick Anthony

Serves 4 as a main course, 6 as an accompaniment

450g (1 lb) greens, shredded

450g (1 lb) broccoli, cut in florets

2 beef tomatoes

Red and green gratin,

with deep-fried

artichoke 'crisps'.

For the cheese sauce

25g (1 oz) butter

25g (1 oz) plain flour

300ml (10 fl oz) milk

100g (4 oz) Cheddar cheese, half diced, half grated

For the garnish

1 tablespoon chopped fresh parsley

bunches of fresh herbs (optional)

For the artichoke crisps

sunflower oil, for deep-frying

225g (8 oz) Jerusalem artichokes, peeled

In a two-tier steamer, place the greens in the bottom section and steam for 8 minutes. Add the broccoli to the top section and steam for 6 minutes. Drain the vegetables and place in a casserole dish.

Meanwhile, halve the tomatoes and put them under a hot grill for 5 minutes, until they are partially cooked. Remove from the grill. Remove the skins, chop the flesh and add to the vegetables.

For the all-in-one cheese sauce, put the butter, flour and milk in a pan, bring to the boil, whisking continuously and simmer for 2 minutes until thickened. Remove from the heat, add the diced cheese and mix well. When smooth, pour the sauce over the vegetables. Sprinkle the grated cheese over and put the dish under a hot grill for 3 minutes, or until the cheese has melted and browned slightly.

Heat the oil for deep-frying in a small pan. Cut the artichokes into thin ribbons with a potato peeler. Deep-fry the ribbons of artichoke until crisp and golden brown. Drain on kitchen paper.

To serve, sprinkle the artichoke crisps on top of the vegetables and around the edge. Garnish with chopped parsley and bunches of fresh herbs, if you like.

Chestnut and Cranberry Casserole ♈

Serves 6-8

Rosemary Moon

1 leek, sliced
1 tablespoon oil
450g (1 lb) peeled chestnuts, fresh or frozen
1 red pepper, seeded and chopped
1 courgette, quartered and sliced thickly
4 sticks celery, chopped roughly
50g (1¾ oz) raisins
1 tablespoon soy sauce
1 tablespoon freshly chopped coriander
1 cinnamon stick, broken
425ml (¾ pint) well-flavoured vegetable stock
225g (8 oz) fresh cranberries

To serve

2 tablespoons demerara sugar
soy sauce to taste
freshly chopped coriander to garnish

This is a dish of surprising flavours – slightly sweet and sour and full of bright colours and textures. The casserole requires very little cooking as the vegetables should still be slightly crunchy and retain their colour. If serving on a bed of brown rice the whole dish can be cooked in the time that it takes to simmer the rice.

Cook the leek in the oil until softened but not browned, then add the chestnuts and stir over the heat until defrosted, if frozen. Add the pepper, courgette, and celery. Stir-fry for 1 minute then stir in all the remaining ingredients except the cranberries and sugar.

Bring the casserole to a boil then simmer gently for 10-15 minutes. Add the cranberries then continue to cook for a further 10 minutes. Remove the cinnamon stick and add the sugar. Stir in extra soy sauce to taste then serve on a bed of boiled rice, garnished with chopped coriander.

Braised Aubergine with Beancurd ♈

Serves 4

Ken Hom

225g (8 oz) Chinese or ordinary aubergine

225g (8 oz) firm, fresh beancurd

3 tablespoons groundnut (peanut) oil

3 large fresh red or green Thai chillies, seeded and sliced

1½ tablespoons fish sauce or light soy sauce

1 tablespoon lime juice

1 teaspoon salt

½ teaspoon freshly ground black pepper

2 teaspoons sugar

handful fresh basil leaves

Small pea-like aubergines are popular in Thailand. They are often used in curries, but the larger, thin Chinese variety is also often used. Here they are stir-fried with beancurd in a vegetarian dish.

If using large aubergines, trim and cut them into 5 x 1cm (2 x ½ inch) diagonal slices. Cut the beancurd gently into 1cm (just under ½ inch) cubes and drain on kitchen paper for 20 minutes.

Heat a wok or large frying pan over high heat until it is hot. Add 2 tablespoons of the oil, and when it is moderately hot, add the aubergine slices and stir-fry for 2 minutes. Then add the beancurd and stir-fry for 3 minutes or until brown. Now add the remaining tablespoon of oil, the chillies, fish sauce, lime juice, salt, pepper and sugar. Bring the mixture to a simmer. Cover and cook for 10 minutes, then stir in the basil leaves.

Turn the mixture on to a warm platter and serve at once.

Glamorgan Sausages with Plum Chutney ♈

Serves 4

150g (5 oz) fresh breadcrumbs
1 small leek, finely chopped
75g (3 oz) Caerphilly cheese, grated
1 tablespoon chopped fresh parsley
salt and freshly ground black pepper
pinch of dry mustard
3 eggs
a little milk
flour
extra breadcrumbs for coating
oil for frying

Gilli Davies

I dare say it was the economics of producing a sausage without any meat in it that made Glamorgan sausages so popular with the Welsh. Containing cheese, breadcrumbs, leeks and herbs, these tasty sausages were mentioned by George Borrow in his book, **Wild Wales,** *written in 1862.*

Mix together the breadcrumbs, leek, cheese, parsley, seasonings and mustard.

Beat together 2 eggs and 1 yolk and use this to bind the mixture, adding a little milk if the mixture is still too dry to hold together.

Divide into 12, roll into sausage shapes and toss in flour.

Beat the remaining egg white until frothy; brush over the sausages, then coat them in the extra breadcrumbs. Chill in the fridge for 20 minutes.

Fry gently in oil until crisp and golden brown on all sides.

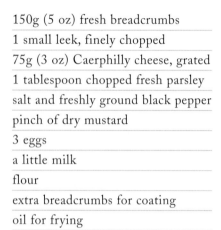

Plum Chutney

1kg (2 lb) plums, stoned

100g (4 oz) dried fruit

1 tablespoon pickling spice

1 teaspoon salt

1 teaspoon ground ginger

1 teaspoon chilli powder

300ml (2 pint) vinegar

350g (12 oz) demerara sugar

Simmer the plums and dried fruit, pickling spice (tied securely in muslin bag – I use the toe from a clean pair of tights or a stocking), salt, ground ginger and chilli powder in a saucepan with just enough vinegar to stop the mixture from burning. Cook gently until the fruit is soft, stirring from time to time.

Add the remaining vinegar and stir in the sugar thoroughly.

Boil the chutney steadily until the mixture is thick. Remove the spice bag.

Pour the chutney into hot clean jars and seal. Serve with Glamorgan Sausages and cold meats such as ham and pork.

Spinach, Ricotta and Egg Filo Pie ♈

Serves 6

1 packet ready-made filo pastry
50ml (2 fl oz) olive oil
500g (18 oz) fresh spinach leaves, washed
175g (6 oz) fresh ricotta cheese
sea salt and black pepper
freshly grated nutmeg
4 medium eggs
1 tablespoon sesame seeds

Thane Prince

*This recipe is an adaptation of cheese **bôrek**, eaten throughout the eastern Mediterranean. It is a tasty vegetarian supper dish.*

Preheat the oven to 200°C/400°F/Gas 6.

Using a pastry brush, brush each of the sheets of filo with olive oil and use them to completely cover the base and sides of a 20cm (8 inch) loose-bottomed, deep flan tin. Don't worry about any overhanging pastry; it can be folded over later.

Place the well-washed spinach in a pan of boiling water, cook for 30 seconds then drain well, pressing as much liquid from the leaves as possible. Chop this roughly. Beat the ricotta with some salt, black pepper and nutmeg.

Brush the base of your pastry case with oil, then cover with half the spinach in an even layer. Spread the ricotta over this and, forming four hollows with a spoon, break the eggs into these. Top with the remaining spinach and carefully fold over the edges of the filo, using extra oiled sheets as necessary to make a flaky top. Brush the top with oil and scatter on the sesame seeds.

Bake the pie in the preheated oven for 20-25 minutes or until golden brown. Serve hot or warm.

A fresh tomato sauce or tossed green salad would go well with this dish.

Vegetable Balti ♈

Serves 4

350g (12 oz) potatoes

2-3 carrots

salt

3 courgettes

250g (9 oz) cup mushrooms

1 yellow sweet pepper

2 medium onions

2 cloves garlic

1 red chilli

4 tablespoons sunflower or other light oil

3 level tablespoons Balti curry paste

1 x 230g tin chopped tomatoes in juice

2 tablespoons chopped fresh coriander

naan bread for serving

Katie Stewart

Special Balti pans are like woks, but you can use a frying pan or traditional wok instead.

Peel and cut the potatoes into bite-sized pieces. Pare and slice the carrots. Add potatoes and carrots to a pan of boiling salted water and simmer for 5 minutes. Trim and thinly slice the courgettes. Trim mushroom stalks level with the cups and leave cups whole. Halve, deseed and finely shred the yellow pepper. Peel and chop the onions. Peel and crush the garlic. Halve, deseed and chop the chilli.

Measure the oil into a 25cm (10 inch) frying pan or wok, add the onions, yellow pepper and chilli and cook gently for 5 minutes until the onion is softened. Stir in the garlic and cook for a moment. Stir in the curry paste, add the remaining vegetables and stir to coat. Add the chopped tomatoes, 150ml (¼ pint) water and the coriander. Bring to a simmer. Reduce the heat to low and cook for 10-15 minutes until the vegetables are tender. Serve as soon as cooked with warmed naan bread for scooping up the vegetables.

Crisp Courgette Flowers Stuffed with Goat's Ricotta, Ratatouille Vinaigrette

Serves 4

Tony Tobin

1 small onion, diced	500g (18 oz) goat's ricotta cheese
2 cloves garlic, crushed	
50ml (2 fl oz) olive oil	1 tbsp tiny capers
1 red pepper, diced	12 courgette flowers
1 courgette, diced	vegetable oil for frying
1 small aubergine, diced	250g (9 oz) plain flour
2 beef tomatoes, cut into tiny dice	60g (2½ oz) cornflour
50ml (2 fl oz) white wine vinegar	300ml (½ pint) lager
salt and freshly ground black pepper	300ml (½ pint) soda water
5 freshly snipped basil leaves	

Sauté the onion and garlic in most of the olive oil until soft. Add the red pepper and cook for a further 5 minutes. Add the courgette and aubergine and cook for 5 minutes. Add the tomatoes and continue cooking for 15 minutes. Add the white wine vinegar and reduce by half. Finish with a little more olive oil and season with salt and pepper. Stir in the chopped basil and put to one side.

Mix the ricotta and tiny capers, and season. Place mix into a piping bag and fill courgette flowers.

Mix the flours with the lager and soda water to make a light batter. Season.

Heat enough oil to make a small deep-fryer. Dust the stuffed flowers with a little extra flour, dip in the batter and quickly fry in the hot oil. Remove and dry on paper towel.

Spoon the ratatouille dressing over each plate and place three fried flowers on each one.

Caramelized Onion and Mustard Tart

Annie Stirk

Serves 4

For the pastry
100g (4 oz) butter
225g (8 oz) wholemeal plain flour
good pinch dry mustard
pinch of salt
50g (2 oz) Cheddar cheese, grated
cold water to mix

Don't be tempted to rush the cooking of the onions – the long, slow cooking gives them the most delicious sweetness.

For the filling
700g (1½ lb) onions, finely sliced
75g (3 oz) unsalted butter
2 eggs, beaten
2 tablespoons grated Parmesan cheese
300ml (½ pint) natural yogurt
salt and freshly ground black pepper

Preheat the oven to 180°C/350°F/Gas 4.

Make the pastry. Rub the butter into the flour until it resembles breadcrumbs. Stir in the mustard, salt and cheese. Season. Bind the mixture together with enough water to form a soft dough. Roll out and line a 23cm (9 inch) flan tin and bake blind for 15 minutes.

Place the onions and butter in a roomy pan. Cook very gently until they are completely softened, browned and caramelized.

Whisk up the eggs, stir in the cheese and the yogurt, and season.

Pile the onions into the pastry case. Pour over the egg and yogurt mixture. Bake for 30-35 minutes until browned and set. Serve with salad and potatoes.

Banana Tarts ♈

Nigel Slater

Makes 4

225g (8 oz) chilled ready-made puff pastry

4 bananas

a little melted butter

a little caster sugar (say 2 tablespoons)

4 tablespoons apricot jam

Thin, flaky tartlets – one

per person – that can also

be made with sliced

peaches, apricots or apples.

Roll the puff pastry out into a large square about 28cm (5 inch) on each side. Using a plate or bowl as a guide, cut four 13cm (11 inch) circles of pastry. Transfer them to a baking sheet and put them in the fridge for 20 minutes.

Remove the pastry. Preheat the oven to 200°C/400°F/Gas 6. Peel the bananas. Slice each one into rounds about twice as thick as a pound coin. Divide the bananas between the pastry, overlapping the slices where necessary. They can be higgledy-piggledy if you like. Brush them, and the pastry edges, with a little melted butter and sprinkle with sugar. Bake in the preheated oven for about 10 minutes until the pastry has puffed up and the bananas are soft.

Spread the apricot jam over the tarts and return to the oven for a further couple of minutes until they are sticky and bubbling. Eat warm with vanilla icecream.

Aromatic Chocolate Cake ♈

Serves 4-6

4-5 cardamom pods

7.5cm (3 inch) piece cinnamon stick

100g (4 oz) darkest chocolate
(containing at least 50% cocoa solids)

2 tablespoons water

4 large eggs

100g (4 oz) light muscovado sugar

1 level teaspoon salt

1 rounded tablespoon cocoa powder

2 rounded tablespoons Greek yogurt

50g (2 oz) stale white bread,
made into breadcrumbs

icing sugar for dusting

Josceline Dimbleby

The smell of spices as you cut into this intense, squidgy cake is, to me, incredibly exciting. The cake is better if made at least a day in advance. It uses breadcrumbs instead of flour, which give it a moist, crumbly texture.

Butter a 15cm (6 inch) cake tin (or a small loaf tin), put a disc of buttered baking parchment on the bottom and dust with flour. Preheat the oven to 180°C/350°F/Gas 4. Extract the seeds from the cardamom pods and break up the cinnamon roughly. Put the spices into a coffee grinder and whizz until finely ground. Put a bowl over a pan of simmering water, making sure the water does not touch the base of the bowl. Put the ground spices into the bowl and leave them for 2-3 minutes, stirring once or twice to release their aroma. Break up the chocolate and add it with the water to the bowl. Turn the heat right down, or off, and stir constantly until the chocolate is melted and smooth. Remove from the heat.

Separate the eggs into 2 bowls, a larger one for the whites. Whisk half the sugar with the egg yolks until pale and very thick, then stir in the melted chocolate, salt, cocoa powder, yogurt and breadcrumbs. Whisk the egg whites until stiff and then gradually fold in the remaining sugar before folding into the chocolate mixture. The mixture should almost be a dropping consistency. If it is very stiff, stir in a tablespoon of water.

Spoon the mixture into the cake tin and cook in the centre of the oven for 30-40 minutes, until it feels firm to a light touch in the centre. Remove from the oven and leave in the tin for 5-10 minutes. Then loosen the edges with a knife and turn out, right-side up, on to a rack to cool. Remove the disc of baking parchment. When cold, wrap in clingfilm and keep in a cool place until needed. Before serving, lightly sprinkle icing sugar through a sieve on top of the cake, as above.

Kheer

Serves 4

400g (14 oz) canned creamed rice
10-12 strands saffron
1 tablespoon sugar
½ teaspoon green cardamoms, ground
¼ nutmeg, freshly grated, to decorate

Pat Chapman

A spicy take on traditional rice pudding.

Simply combine everything in a bowl but the nutmeg and allow to stand for at least an hour in the fridge, while the saffron infuses.

Sprinkle with nutmeg and serve.

Instant Banoffi Pie ♈

Serves 4

250g (8 oz) digestive biscuits
(preferably a brand that is not too sweet)

125g (4 oz) unsalted butter, melted

4 small or 2 large bananas

50g (2 oz) unsalted butter

2 teaspoons soft brown sugar

2 tablespoons brandy

125g (4 oz) Toblerone, Mars Bar,
Bounty, Dairy Milk, Galaxy, Caramel,
Hershey, Milky Bar or best-quality
'real' chocolate, melted

300ml (½ pint) whipping cream,
whipped and chilled

Valentina Harris

A gorgeous, rich,

creamy indulgence for

everyone who loves

sweet things.

Crumble the biscuits finely and mix with the melted butter to make
a paste.

Line a 23cm (9 inch) spring-form cake tin or loose-bottomed flan tin
with the biscuit mixture and chill.

Slice the bananas in half lengthways and fry gently with the rest of the
butter, sprinkling with the sugar. Pour the brandy over the bananas,
ignite and wait for the flames to subside.

Pour the contents of the pan over the biscuit base.

Melt the chocolate of your choice in a bowl over a saucepan of
simmering water.

When you are ready to serve, slide the banana base out of the tin on to
a plate and pour the warm chocolate over it.

Cover with the cream and serve at once.

Home-made Eccles Cakes ♈

Makes 4 cakes

225g (8 oz) frozen bought puff pastry, thawed

50g (2 oz) currants

25g (1 oz) soft light brown sugar

25g (1 oz) butter, softened

a pinch of ground cinnamon

the finely grated zest of 1 orange

1 egg white

granulated sugar

Gary Rhodes

Eccles cakes are a classic for our corner-shop bakers and for us to eat! So, why not have a go at making your own? They really are very simple to make and even more delicious to eat.

Preheat the oven to 200°C/400°F/Gas 6.

Roll out the pastry to about 2mm (⅛ inch) thick. Mix together the currants, soft brown sugar, butter, cinnamon and grated zest of orange.

Cut four 15cm (6 inch) discs of pastry. Divide the filling between each of the discs, placing a dome of mix in the centre of each one. Brush the edges of the pastry with water and gather all together, creating a 'bag' effect. Press the pastry together, cutting off any excess. The 'bag' can now be turned over on to a lightly floured board and softly rolled so that the pastry thins a little to reveal the currants, keeping a good circular shape. Repeat this simple process for the remaining three.

Brush each cake with egg white and sprinkle with granulated sugar. Score the tops with a sharp knife, making three or four lines. Rest in the fridge for 15-20 minutes. Bake on buttered greaseproof paper for 25 minutes until rich, golden and crispy.

The eccles cakes can be eaten as a pastry cake, warm or cold. However, they can also be served as a dessert with custard, clotted cream, vanilla ice-cream, or the lot!

Old-fashioned Pancakes with Orange ♈

Makes 12 pancakes

100g (3½ oz) plain flour, sifted

pinch of salt

2 eggs

140g (4½ oz) caster sugar

300ml (½ pint) milk

45g (1½ oz) butter

6 oranges

200ml (7 fl oz) water

2 teaspoons cornflour

2 tablespoons Grand Marnier

icing sugar for dusting

4 sprigs of mint

Anton Edelmann

There is nothing more comforting than this traditional, sweet dessert with a deliciously zesty finish.

Mix the flour and salt in a large bowl, then add the eggs, 4 tablespoons of the sugar and about a quarter of the milk and mix to a thick batter. Slowly add the rest of the milk to give a thin pouring batter. If there are any lumps in it, pass it through a fine sieve.

Melt the butter in a pan until it begins to foam and then whisk half of it into the batter. Leave to rest in a cool place for 15 minutes.

Meanwhile, pare the zest from one orange with a vegetable peeler and cut it into long, thin strips. Blanch and drain. To caramelize it, dissolve the remaining sugar in the water over a gentle heat and then bring to the boil. Add the orange zest and boil gently for about 10 minutes, until the liquid had reduced to a pale golden caramel. Add about 2 tablespoons of cold water to stop the cooking, then remove from the heat and leave to cool.

Remove all the skin and white pith from 2 of the oranges and cut out the segments from between the membranes. Do this over a bowl to catch the juice and squeeze out the juice from the membranes once you have removed all the segments. Squeeze the juice from the remaining 4 oranges and add to the juice from the segmented oranges.

Mix 1 tablespoon of the orange juice with the cornflour. Bring the remaining orange juice to the boil and stir in the cornflour mixture. Cook, stirring, for 1-2 minutes, until lightly thickened. Remove from the heat and stir in the Grand Marnier. If the oranges are tart, you can add a little sugar.

Preheat the oven to 200°C/400°F/Gas 6. Heat a 15cm (6 inch) diameter non-stick omelette pan, brush with a little of the remaining melted butter, then ladle in enough batter to cover the base of the pan in a thin layer, tilting the pan so the batter spreads evenly. Cook for 30 seconds over a medium-high heat until browned, then turn over and cook for a further 30 seconds. Continue making them in this way until all the batter is used up. There should be 12 pancakes.

Fold each pancake into quarters, place them on a baking sheet, drizzle with orange sauce and reheat in the oven for 5-10 minutes. Be careful they do not dry out at the edges. Warm the caramelized orange zest and remove from the sugar syrup.

Reheat the sauce and pour enough on to each serving plate to cover the base. Dust the pancakes generously with icing sugar and arrange 3 on each plate. Decorate with the orange segments, caramelized zest and mint.

Treacle Spice Traybake ♈

Makes about 15-20 slices

225g (8 oz) soft margarine

175g (6 oz) caster sugar

225g (8 oz) black treacle

275g (10 oz) self-raising flour

2 teaspoons baking powder

2 teaspoons mixed spice

4 eggs

4 tablespoons milk

3 bulbs of stem ginger, chopped finely

For the icing

75g (3 oz) icing sugar, sieved

about 2 tablespoons stem ginger syrup from the jar

2 bulbs stem ginger, finely chopped

Mary Berry

This is one for those who like the rich flavour of treacle in baking. Don't be too worried if the traybake dips in the centre – it means you were a little generous with the treacle. To make it easy, weigh the treacle on top of the sugar in the scale pan, adding the two weights together.

Preheat the oven to 180°C/350°F/Gas 4.

Grease and base line a 30 x 23cm (12 x 9 inch) small roasting tin with foil.

Measure all the ingredients into a large bowl and beat well for about 2 minutes until well blended. Turn the mixture into the prepared tin and level the top.

Bake in the preheated oven for approximately 40 minutes or until the cake has shrunk from the sides and springs back when pressed in the centre with your fingertips. Remove from the oven; allow to cool in the tin.

Mix the icing sugar with the syrup until coating consistency, and spread over the top of the cake. Sprinkle with chopped stem ginger. If preferred, dust with sifted icing sugar.

Vanilla Cream with Strawberries Poached in Elderflower

Serves 4

For the vanilla cream

1 litre (1¾ pints) whipping cream

150g (5 oz) caster sugar

2 vanilla pods, split

3 gelatine leaves, dissolved in a little water

For the strawberries

25ml (1 fl oz) elderflower cordial

200ml (7 fl oz) water

50g (2 oz) caster sugar

1 punnet of strawberries, cut into halves

Paul Heathcote

This is a beautiful summer dish, perfect for when strawberries are at their best.

To make the vanilla cream, bring the cream, sugar and split vanilla pods to the boil. Remove from the heat and add the dissolved gelatine. Stir to mix and thoroughly dissolve, leave to cool, then pour into ramekins. Chill until set, about 4 hours.

To poach the strawberries, bring the elderflower cordial, water and sugar to the boil. Add the strawberries and gently simmer for 2 minutes. Allow to cool.

To serve, turn the vanilla creams out on to serving plates, and surround with a few poached strawberries and a little of the syrup.

No-nonsense Sherry Trifle ♈

Serves 6 generously

225g (8 oz) trifle sponges

150g (5½ oz) best-quality
raspberry jam

150ml (¼ pint) dry or medium sherry

850ml (1½ pints) custard (made
according to the instructions on the
packet), cooled slightly

300ml (½ pint) double cream,
whipped until stiff

flaked almonds to decorate

Richard Cawley

My mother's recipe –

the best – never fails to

win compliments.

Slice each sponge cake in half across and spread thickly with jam.
Arrange jam side up in the bottom of a glass bowl and pour over
the sherry.

Pour over the slightly cooled custard, prodding the sponges a little with
a fork to ensure that the custard seeps down through every space to the
bottom of the bowl. Chill until set.

Cover with whipped cream and decorate with almonds.

Shortbread Ice-cream with Sticky Bananas ♈

1 x 500ml (18 fl oz) carton good-quality vanilla ice-cream

100g (4 oz) shortbread, roughly chopped into large chunks

4 bananas, peeled and halved

lemon juice

75g (3 oz) dark muscovado sugar

75g (3 oz) unsalted butter

150ml (¼ pint) double cream

Sue Lawrence

Use thick shortbread fingers for this recipe, not thin petticoat tail rounds; you will need about five fingers.

Soften the ice-cream for about 20 minutes, then stir in the shortbread. Spoon into a dish, cover and refreeze for about 20 minutes.

Place the bananas in a shallow dish and sprinkle with a little lemon juice.

Place the sugar, butter and cream in a saucepan and bring slowly to the boil. Bubble away for about 3 minutes then pour all over the bananas.

Place in a preheated oven (220°C/425°F/Gas 7) for 10-15 minutes until sticky and piping hot. Eat with a scoop of shortbread ice-cream.

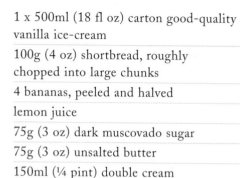

Flat Blueberry Tart ♈

Serves 6-8

350g (12 oz) shortcrust pastry

caster sugar for rolling

280g (10 oz) cream cheese

juice and grated rind of 1 large orange

2 tablespoons icing sugar

280g (10 oz) blueberries

icing sugar for dusting

Lesley Waters

A stunning-looking tart

that requires very little

effort, combining fresh fruit,

cream cheese and pastry.

Blueberries are not the only

fruit – try fresh apricots,

peaches or strawberries, too.

Preheat the oven to 200°C/400°F/Gas 6. Line a baking tray with non-stick baking parchment.

On a clean surface, using caster sugar in place of flour, roll out the pastry until approximately 5mm (¼ inch) thick. Using a large dinner plate, cut out a neat round about 23cm (9 inches) in diameter and carefully place on to the lined baking tray. Prick the pastry all over and crimp or fork the edges.

Bake the pastry in the oven for 10-12 minutes, or until cooked and biscuit coloured. Allow the pastry to cool completely before carefully transferring to a serving plate.

In a small bowl beat the cream cheese with the orange juice and grated rind, adding icing sugar to taste. Spread this mixture over the pastry base leaving a 2.5cm (1 inch) border clear.

Top the orange cream with the blueberries and lightly dust with icing sugar. Serve at once.

Yorkshire Curd Tart ♈

Serves 4-6

175g (6 oz) shortcrust pastry

1 lemon

2 teaspoons mixed peel

2 eggs

250g (8 oz) curd or cottage cheese

50g (2 oz) sugar

50g (2 oz) currants

¼ teaspoon ground cinnamon

¼ teaspoon grated nutmeg

Susan Brookes

This traditional tart is usually eaten cold or at room temperature. Serve it in slices, with cream if liked.

Roll out the pastry on a lightly floured surface and use to line a 20cm (8 inch) round flan tin or pie dish.

Finely grate the rind from the lemon, then finely chop the mixed peel. Beat the eggs in a large mixing bowl, add all the other ingredients including the lemon rind and mixed peel and mix well. Pour the mixture into the pastry case.

Bake in a preheated oven, 180°C/350°F/Gas 4, for 35-50 minutes or until the filling is golden and set. Serve with cream or ice-cream, if liked.

RECIPES

Darina Allen for Pea and Coriander Soup from *A Year at Ballymaloe Cookery School* (Kyle Cathie, 1997), **Patrick Anthony** for Michelle's Mélange from *Ready Steady Cook 2* (BBC Books, 1996), **Jane Asher** for Salmon Fish Cakes with Quick Tartare Sauce, **Michael Barry** for Salmon en Croûte with Lemon Cream Sauce first seen on *Food & Drink* and published in *BBC Good Food* magazine, **Mary Berry** for Treacle Spice Traybake from *Ultimate Cakes* (BBC Books, 1994), **Raymond Blanc** for Curried Cream of Cauliflower Soup with Coriander Purée, Red Mullet with Green Olive Tapenade and Courgettes, and Glazed Lamb Shanks from *Blanc Vite* (Headline, 1998), **Susan Brookes** for Yorkshire Curd Tart from *Truly Wonderful Puddings & Desserts* (Hamlyn, 1995), **Ross Burden** for Hake in Serrano Ham with Capers and Saffron Pasta from *At Home with Ross Burden* (Metro Books, 1998), **Antonio Carluccio** for Sardines Beccafico-style from *BBC Good Food* magazine, **Richard Cawley** for No-nonsense Sherry Trifle from *Fast Fab Food* (Headline, 1997), **Pat Chapman** for Kheer from *Pat Chapman's Curry Bible*, reproduced by permission of Hodder & Stoughton, **Gilli Davies** for Glamorgan Sausages with Plum Chutney from *A Taste of Wales* (Pavilion, 1995), **Josceline Dimbleby** for Aromatic Chocolate Cake from *Josceline Dimbleby's Complete Cookbook* (HarperCollins, 1997) and Spicy Shepherd's Pie with Spinach and Sesame Seeds, from *BBC Good Food* magazine, **Anton Edelmann** for Old-fashioned Pancakes with Orange from *Fast Feasts* (HarperCollins, 1995), **Hugh Fearnley-Whittingstall** for Scallops Cha Cha Cha and Fresh Goat's Cheese with Hedgerow Herbs from *A Cook on the Wild Side* (Boxtree, 1997), **Peter Gordon** for Salad of Watermelon, Feta and Toasted Pumpkin Seeds, and Grilled Mackerel with a Sweet Chilli Glaze on Mixed Bean Salad from *The Sugar Club Cookbook*, reproduced by permission of Hodder & Stoughton, **Sophie Grigson** for Penne alla Vodka con Caviale and Crab Cocktail from *Fish* (Headline, 1997), **Ainsley Harriott** for Mixed Mediterranean Salad, Sinhalese Pasta Prawns with Lemon and Grilled Swordfish with Green Lentil Salad from *BBC Good Food* magazine, **Valentina Harris** for Instant Banoffi Pie from *Who'll Do the Pudding?* (Broadcasting Support Services, 1977), **Paul Heathcote** for Vanilla Cream with Strawberries Poached in Elderflower, **Ken Hom** for Braised Aubergine with Beancurd and Crispy Wontons from *Ken Hom Cooks Thai* (Headline, 1999), **Sue Lawrence** for Shortbread Ice-cream with Sticky Bananas, first published in Sue Lawrence's column in *The Sunday Times*, **Nigella Lawson** for Noodles with Spring Onions, Shitake Mushrooms and Mangetouts from *How to Eat* (Chatto & Windus, 1998), **James Martin** for Leftover Chicken with Mint, Chickpea and Lemon Salad from *Eating In with James Martin* (Mitchell Beazley, 1998), **Rosemary Moon** for Chestnut and Cranberry Casserole from *High-fibre Cooking* (Quintet, 1996), **Anton Mosimann** for Tomato, Mozzarella and Basil Terrine from *Essential Mosimann* (Ebury, 1993), **Orlando Murrin** for Pine Nut, Spinach and Two Cheese Pasta Salad from *BBC Good Food* magazine, **Nick Nairn** for Mussel and Saffron Soup from *Island Harvest* (BBC Books, 1998), **Andrew Nutter** for Parmesan-crusted Salmon with a Mussel and Coriander Chowder from *Utter Nutter* (Bantam, 1997), **Jamie Oliver** for My Perfect Roast Chicken from *The Naked Chef* (Michael Joseph, 1999), **Jennifer Paterson** for Beef Stew with Red Wine and Brandy from *Jennifer Paterson's Seasonal Recipes* (Headline, 1997), **Marguerite Patten** for Vegetable and Cheese Pâté, **Thane Prince** for Spinach, Ricotta and Egg Filo Pie from *Thane Prince's Simply Good Food* (Headline, 1999), **Paul and Jeanne Rankin** for Glazed Chilli Quail with Bok Choy from *Hot Food* (Mitchell Beazley, 1997), **Gary Rhodes** for Slow-honey-roast Duck and Home-made Eccles Cakes from *Fabulous Food* (BBC Books, 1997), **Claudia Roden** for Shakshouka from the *Good Food Show* brochure (1996), **Ruth Rogers and Rose Gray** for Farfalle with Mint, Prosciutto and Peas, and Conchiglie with Ricotta and Rocket from *The River Cafe Cookbook* (Ebury, 1995), **Andrew Sargent** for Roast Vine Tomato, Aged Balsamic and New Season Olive Oil, **Nigel Slater** for Hot Thai Stir-fry and Banana Tarts from *Real Cooking* (Michael Joseph, 1997), **Delia Smith** for Corned-Beef Hash with Fried Eggs from *Delia's How To Cook Book One* (BBC Books, 1998) and French Onion Soup from *Delia Smith's Winter Collection* (BBC Books, 1995), **Rick Stein** for La Mouclade from *Rick Stein's Seafood Odyssey* (BBC Books, 1999), Sautéed Red Mullet with Parsley, Garlic and Spaghettini from *Rick Stein's Fruits of the Sea* (BBC Books, 1997), **Katie Stewart** for Vegetable Balti, **Annie Stirk** for Caramelized Onion and Mustard Tart, **Tony Tobin** for Crisp Courgette Flowers Stuffed with Goat's Ricotta, Ratatouille Vinaigrette, **Brian Turner** for Braised Ham with Mustard Sauce from *Out to Lunch with Brian Turner*, published by Anglia Television Ltd, 1997, **Phil Vickery** for Lemon Sole with Grapes and White Wine Sauce from *Who'll Do the Pudding?* (Broadcasting Support Services, 1977), **Lesley Waters** for Flat Blueberry Tart from *Broader than Beans* (Headline, 1998), **Antony Worrall Thompson** for Thai Green Chicken Curry and Risotto of Greens, Garlic, Anchovies and Capers from *The ABC of AWT* (Headline, 1998) and **Kevin Woodford** for Pork Meatballs with Coriander Couscous from *Big Kevin, Little Kevin* (Ebury, 1999).

PHOTOGRAPHS

Georgia Glynn Smith: Crab Cocktail from Sophie Grigson's *Fish* (Headline, 1997)

Anna Hodgson: No-nonsense Sherry Trifle from Richard Cawley's *Fast Fab Food* (Headline, 1997)

Peter Knab: Crispy Wontons and Braised Aubergine with Beancurd from *Ken Hom Cooks Thai* (Headline, 1999); Curried Cream of Cauliflower Soup with Coriander Purée, Glazed Lamb Shanks, Red Mullet with Green Olives Tapenade and Courgettes from Raymond Blanc's *Blanc Vite* (Headline, 1998)

Jess Koppel: Peter Gordon's Watermelon, Feta and Toasted Pumpkin Seeds; Ainsley Harriott's Sinhalese Pasta Prawns with Lemon; Rick Stein's La Mouclade; Anton Edelmann's Old-fashioned Pancakes with Orange; Josceline Dimbleby's Aromatic Chocolate Cake

Steve Lee: Thai Green Chicken Curry, and Risotto of Greens, Garlic, Anchovies and Capers from Antony Worrall Thompson's *The ABC of AWT* (Headline, 1998)

Roger Stowell: Spinach, Ricotta and Egg Filo Pie from *Thane Prince's Simply Good Food* (Headline, 1998)

COVER PHOTOGRAPHS

Nic Barlow (Anton Mosimann)
Sian Irvine (Ross Burden and Patrick Anthony)
Miki Duisterhof (Delia Smith)
Kevin Summers (Nigel Slater)
Jean Cazals (Jamie Oliver and Peter Gordon)
By kind permission of Channel 4 (Hugh Fearnley-Whittingstall)
Renzo Mazzolini (Nick Nairn)
Richard Haughton (Thane Prince)
Peter Knab (Ken Hom and Raymond Blanc)
Anna Hodgson (Richard Cawley)
Tim MacPherson (Lesley Waters and Jennifer Paterson)
Simon Wheeler (Sophie Grigson)
Dan Burn-Forti (Antony Worrall Thompson)
Georgia Glynn Smith (Phil Vickery)
David Williams (Brian Turner)
Derry Moore (Rose Gray and Ruth Rogers)
Tony Timmington (Antonio Carluccio)
David Loftus (Andrew Sargent)
Geoff Wilkinson (Orlando Murrin)

Gary Moyes (Ainsley Harriott)
Tracy Gibbs (Paul Heathcote)
Harry Williams (Gilli Davies)
Colin Poole (Pat Chapman)
Cati Majtenyi (Annie Stirk)
Debbie Major (Rick Stein)
Red Saunders (Claudia Roden)
Khara Pringle (Paul and Jeanne Rankin)
Apertures (Rosemary Moon)
Alan Olley (Jane Asher)
Andy Lane (Sue Lawrence)
John Green (Kevin Woodford)
Tim Winter (Nigella Lawson)
Tim MacPherson (Gary Rhodes)
By kind permission of
Granada Television (Susan Brookes)
Robin Matthews (Mary Berry)
Leigh Simpson (Tony Tobin)

SOPHIE GRIGSON'S ACKNOWLEDGEMENTS

Everyone who has been approached to help with this project has been enormously, though unsurprisingly, keen to help. I'd particularly like to thank Mary Clyne, who is actually the prime-mover behind the project, as well as Heather Holden-Brown, Esther Jones, Ros Ellis, Rebecca Purtell, Liz Allen, Bryone Picton, Lizzie White, Jo Roberts-Miller, Juliana Lessa, Lorraine Jerram, Jon Morgan and all those at Headline who have thrown themselves into producing the book in record time. Special thanks to Carole McDonald at Design/Section for making the book so beautiful. Jess Koppel, with the support of food stylists, Lyn Rutherford and Roisin Nield, has taken some beautiful photographs especially for *Cooks for Kosovo*, making this far more than just another charity cookbook. Fifty-one television cooks and chefs have donated recipes impressively speedily, and have given the project great support. Thanks again to all of them.

HEADLINE'S ACKNOWLEDGEMENTS

Thank you, first and foremost, to Sophie Grigson and Mary Clyne, without whom the project would not have been conceived and whose generosity of spirit has never ceased to amaze us.

All the people who have been involved in this project have given their services for free or at a reduced rate. Without such enthusiasm and understanding, Headline wouldn't have made it. We would like to give a huge thanks to them all: Head Design, Design/Section, Radstock Repro, Butler and Tanner, Precision Publishing Papers, Letterpart, Slatter Anderson, Clark Stephen, LDA. As ever, Susan Fleming has been a complete star – this time providing much-needed advice and editing at the very last minute. The fifty-one cooks and chefs, who have donated recipes without so much as a bat of an eyelid, and their agents have been so kind to take time out from their busy schedules to be part of this truly worthwhile project. A special thank you, also, to the Bluebird in London's King's Road for allowing us – at no cost at all – to take over the restaurant for one night in July, so that we can launch the book with a major fund-raising event.